Tyler Feller's faith and love a
challenges us to see our challenges as opportunities and shows
us authentically how to grow through them. *Don't Stop* points
us beyond ourselves to the God who never gives up on us.

Jud Wilhite, senior pastor, Central Church; author, *Pursued*

Don't Stop offers timely and practical tools to see your future with a renewed mind and hope. It will inspire you to dream the dreams God put inside you, to get over yourself, and to keep moving. You can't steer a parked car.

Will Hart, CEO, Iris Global; author, *GodRunner: Your Place in God's Big Story*

In *Don't Stop*, Tyler Feller reminds us that we have a God who is always working behind the scenes of our life. So many people we minister to through our television programs at TCT are looking and searching for hope. *Don't Stop* delivers the encouragement they need to continue to run the race before them and unashamedly dream big with God.

Tom Nolan, president, TCT Network

No matter where you are, no matter what pile of fear, pain, or pride you are under, the God who sees you knows your name—your true self. In chapter 13, Tyler creatively shares how you are the pearl of great price. The Holy Trinity is moving heaven and earth to bring you home. Don't stop!

Brad Robison, MD, board-certified psychiatrist; author, *The Shack Study Guide: Healing for Your Journey through Loss, Trauma, and Pain* with Wm. Paul Young

I've had a front-row seat to watching Tyler courageously tackle difficult circumstances. He listens to God and follows the Spirit's leading every day. He's been a key influencer at Intentional Churches and is a great inspiration to each church he serves. In *Don't Stop*, Tyler pragmatically shares how you follow God every day and end up in places you never dreamed!

Bart Rendel, cofounder, Intentional Churches;
author, *Intentional Churches*

Tyler, very young yet very dynamic, has demonstrated to thousands of people from all walks of life and all ages in the Philippines what it means to rise above challenges through his inspiring messages and lifestyle. We are blessed to have hosted him at our college several times, and we invite him each year to be featured as a keynote speaker for our leadership conference. *Don't Stop* will now become a staple of encouragement for our faculty and students. I wish we had this sooner.

Dr. Joyce Porcadilla, president,
General Baptist Bible College, Philippines

don't stop

Learn to See Your Failures and Struggles as Opportunities

TYLER FELLER

Foreword by Randy Clark

BroadStreet
PUBLISHING

BroadStreet Publishing® Group, LLC
Savage, Minnesota, USA
BroadStreetPublishing.com

9781424567249 (softcover)
9781424567256 (ebook)

Stock or custom editions of BroadStreet Publishing titles may be purchased in bulk for educational, business, ministry, fundraising, or sales promotional use. For information, please email orders@broadstreetpublishing.com.

Cover and interior by Garborg Design Works | garborgdesign.com

Printed in China

24 25 26 27 28 5 4 3 2 1

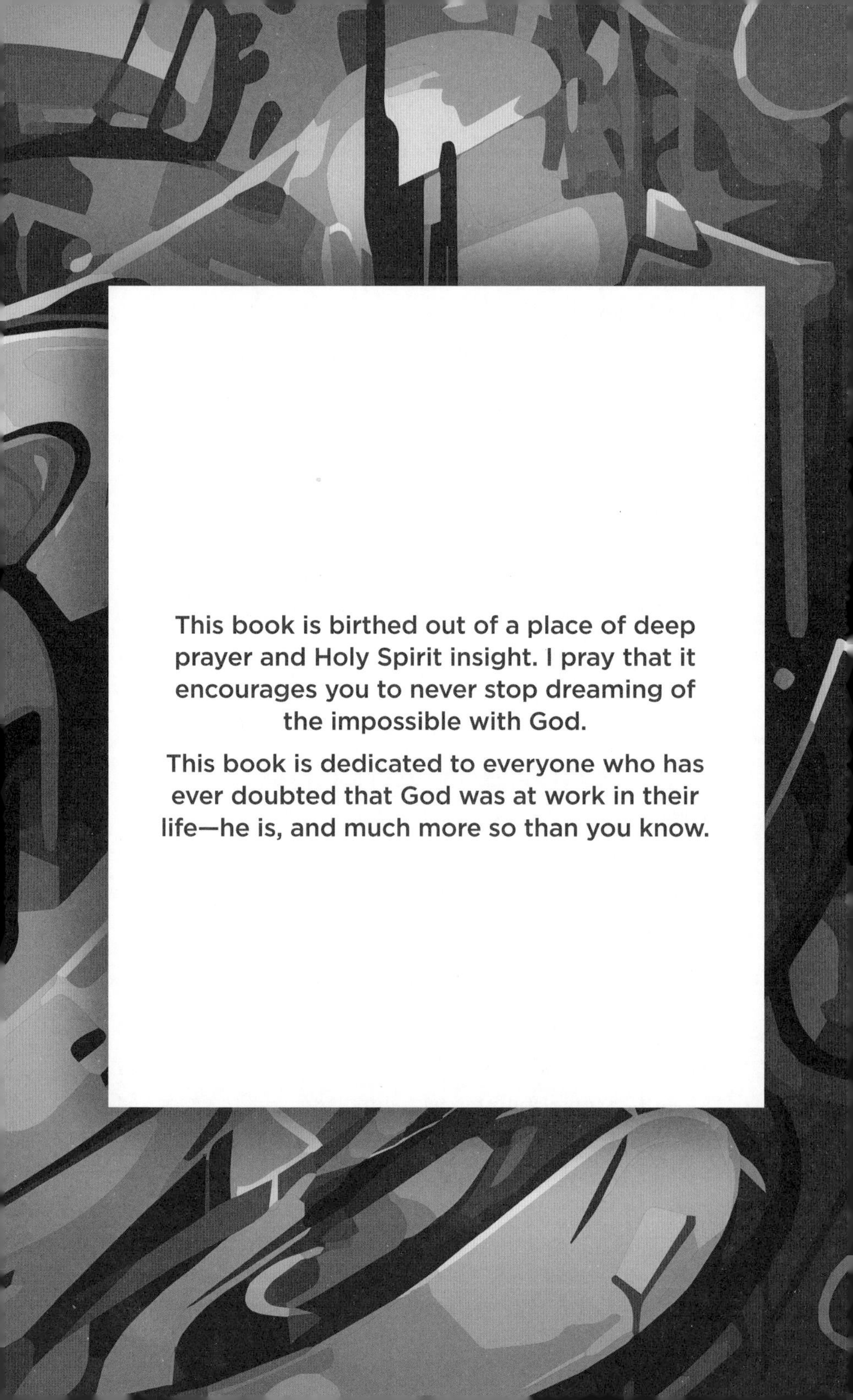

This book is birthed out of a place of deep prayer and Holy Spirit insight. I pray that it encourages you to never stop dreaming of the impossible with God.

This book is dedicated to everyone who has ever doubted that God was at work in their life—he is, and much more so than you know.

contents

foreword

This book is exactly what we need for the season we are in. The Enemy has used every tactic to keep great people away from the dreams that God has placed inside them. *Don't Stop* unleashes a game plan to release the supernatural favor and voice of God into your situation.

In the summer of 1993, I was on the verge of a nervous breakdown. I had planted a Vineyard Church in St. Louis, Missouri, in 1986, and seven years had seen it grow to about three hundred people. It had not been easy. After the first eleven months, I had only eleven people. Perhaps that isn't too bad for starting a church from scratch, and even three hundred people in seven years might be impressive to some. Still, I was disappointed and discouraged because I had come to St. Louis eagerly anticipating much more.

Even though we saw over ninety baptisms that year, I thought I was a failure because we had not seen any healings or impartation. What had happened to God? Where did he go? It was painful to be a pastor in dryness when nothing seemed to be happening in those two areas.

After a divine phone call from my friend Jeff, I knew I needed to attend a conference led by Rodney Howard-Browne. According to Jeff, Rodney had said that he would pray for one thousand men at his meetings, and those men would then go out to bring revival through miracles, signs, and wonders. That night I sat up until 3 a.m. crying. I said, "Lord, I want to be one of those thousand. I'll do anything. I'll pay any price, just use me." I drove to Tulsa where Rodney was speaking, and God powerfully touched me when Rodney laid hands on me and prayed.

The very next Sunday in my church, the spirit of God fell powerfully. I was asked to speak at a regional pastor's meeting for Vineyard Churches, and again the presence of God fell. As a result of this meeting, John Arnott invited me to Toronto, where God would use me to birth a revival that is now known as the Father's Blessing.

My desperation to seek God and my determination not to quit are what led me to the next level. If you have failures, unmet expectations, or unrealized dreams, this book is for you. Tyler lays out a simple blueprint for you to see God where you haven't before. You will be encouraged, inspired, and ready to achieve more with God. Don't stop.

Randy Clark
Founder, Global Awakening

INTRODUCTION

the barracuda versus the goldfish

I once heard a story about an aquarium owner.

I don't know why, but he put a barracuda in the same tank as a goldfish. Under normal circumstances, a barracuda would devour a goldfish in no time. But this tank didn't have the normal conditions.

A clear glass partition separated the goldfish from the barracuda. Like a snake ready to strike, the barracuda circled round and round until he felt the moment was right—and then *bam*! He smacked the glass wall like someone trying to walk through a recently cleaned sliding-glass door. There was no meal for him this time.

A couple of hours later, he tried again to no avail. And the next day, he failed again. The aquarium owner got used to the thud sound of the barracuda hitting the partition.

Then there was a day when the owner heard no sound coming from the tank. He checked and saw that both the goldfish and barracuda were doing fine. It was as if the barracuda had given up.

So the owner removed the partition. And the barracuda could have had success, if he just tried one more time. But he never did.

What if you are just one more try away from the breakthrough you have been praying for?

One more job application to land your dream career. One more creative idea to receive validation and fulfillment. One more invitation until the lost family member whom you lose sleep over decides to attend church. One more prayer to God until all heaven breaks loose in your life. So many times, I think we give up when we aren't called to give up. We are called to keep going.

One.

More.

Time.

And you might find out that the barrier that has held you back in the past is now gone.

Don't stop.

PART ONE

you have made it this far, so don't stop now

If you have a pulse, you have a purpose. There is still more you can accomplish for God. Keep going. Don't stop.

CHAPTER 1

a ten-year-old president

I grew up in a beyond-rural small town of fewer than five hundred people. Most people owned at least five different kinds of animals. Some animals were friends, but most were food. Gravel was just as common as blacktop, and each family usually had at least one truck. In the summer, baseball and the Current River were kings.

Dreams were small, and for the most part, that was what people wanted. I remember feeling different. I dreamed about being the president of the United States.

When I was in fourth grade, Al Gore and George Bush (the younger one) were each vying to become the commander in chief. Every aspect of something so public was intriguing to me, particularly how two people were each able to get 50 percent of the nation to believe in them. My family seemed to support Gore, but I was drawn to Bush. He seemed real to me, and I felt like he genuinely cared.

My school was staging an election to teach us about the Electoral College, campaigns, and voting. Each class throughout the grades nominated several students to run for president. The first obstacle was getting the class to choose you.

After I got my class to choose me as their presidential candidate, I was able to move on to persuading the entire student body. Each of those who made it through their class primary was set to travel from grade to grade, class to class, and perform a speech that would seal the deal as the next US president. On the day of the actual countrywide election, our student body conducted its own election. The winner did not really win anything, as it was a learning experience more than anything else. For me, it was a moment to transpose what had so intrigued me on TV to my own life.

In a landslide, I was elected the president of the United States. I was ecstatic with the results and could not believe they had been so overwhelmingly in my favor. After all, it took a very long time to really know who won between Gore and Bush. They gave me the cardboard ballot box, constructed by a teacher, that contained all the votes that the students had cast. Several times over the next few years I sat in my closet, where I stored this big box, and performed recounts of my own. Each time I allowed my confidence in my strategy to spur me on to develop even more.

Some months later, it was career day, and we got to dress up as the occupation we hoped to have in the future. Since I was just elected president, it made sense to dress up as that. I had been putting the Missouri and US flags on and taking them off the school flagpole every day and learned how to properly fold them. I even formed a team to help and started to delegate responsibilities pertaining to the flags. Every day, as the flag went up and came back down, I thought about myself sitting in Jefferson City and governing the Show-Me State.

They took pictures of us in our career outfits, and our guidance counselor happened to be walking by. I did not really know her or even what a counselor was. I just thought she was nice. She stopped at each of the kids and read the name tags that displayed the title of their career choice if their outfit was subtle. When she got to me, she mistakenly said, "Preacher," as she read it, instead of president. I did not correct her because I was embarrassed. But I was also inspired.

The embarrassment came from not feeling good enough, even at that age, to be a preacher. Sensing that maybe I was not too bad to be a preacher, I felt new life. For the first time, I started to dream about what that would be like. I went to church every Sunday and had always regarded pastors with the highest level of respect. To me, their influence was greater than that of the president of the United States. Unfortunately, from my experience with preachers, all I knew was fire and brimstone. It made me think preachers were perfect. I also thought they had to be.

I took off my president tag and let people guess what I was for the rest of the day. Over the years, I would wrestle with my path, but that moment of getting my photo taken did something to me. I had taken off the label that I had assigned to myself. I allowed myself to dream big and without shame.

dream big

To this day, I always ask people what their dream job is. I do this because it tells me a lot about a person. Recently, while I was getting my hair cut, I asked my stylist, Stevie, if this was her dream job. She laughed at me. She laughed a lot.

"Absolutely not!" she said.

How was I supposed to know? I pressed, now intrigued and really wanting to know, "Well, what is your dream job?"

She replied, "We don't have enough time to get into all that." I could sense that she was not happy with her life or her vocation, though she was good at it.

How terrible it would feel to live a life in which we are not doing what we feel like we are supposed to be doing. Or even worse, to feel like we don't have a purpose at all. God actually created us with intent. We have something to accomplish, a mission perhaps, that we are uniquely designed for.

My heart broke for Stevie, and I changed the subject. I also left her a good tip.

God's thoughts about you

Sometimes people don't live out their purpose because they are afraid to dream. I can make a compelling case that it is sinful not to dream big dreams with our lives. This book is centered around you discovering that for yourself. God designed you for something only you can accomplish. Finding your purpose is the answer to a plethora of life's anxieties.

Think about your walk with God like this: out of all the beautiful places on earth—the waterfalls, beaches, snow-covered mountains—you are his treasured possession. You are the apple of his eye. He's crazy about you.

Before you were born and while in your mother's womb, God breathed life into you and declared you to be fearfully and wonderfully made. The Creator knitted you together, you as his creation. And when you were born and took your first breath, God was the one who ushered in the oxygen to your lungs. The thoughts he has of you, good thoughts, are more numerous than the stars in the sky or the sands in the sea.

And that all takes place in your first second of life. How much more he has for you! The plans he has for you are for a hope and a future, for you to prosper and not be harmed. Somewhere along the way in this life, we stop dreaming. And without dreaming, we stop living in the vast potential that God has for our life.

Or as a saying often attributed to Ben Franklin says, "Most men die from the neck up by the age of twenty-five because they stop dreaming."

famous dreamer

Joseph was one of the most famous dreamers in the Bible. You can read the story of his dreams beginning in Genesis 37. He was given a lot of favor from his family, and God revealed something amazing to him in one of his dreams.

In this dream, Joseph pictured a scene in which he was in a position of influence ruling a nation. His brothers, who already held a little animosity toward him, actually bowed down to him in this dream. Joseph seems like he was a pretty humble guy, but what I love is that he was able to share his dream with his family unashamedly.

Of course, his older brothers did not like the idea of them bowing down to him. This didn't sit right with them. Culturally, the little brother was supposed to bow to the older brothers, not the other way around. They were also fed up with the special treatment he received as the golden boy of the family. They decided he deserved to be punished. At first, they actually thought maybe they would kill him. Luckily, one of the brothers was smart enough to know that this was not the best route. Instead, they found a big hole, threw Joseph in it, and waited until a caravan of merchants came by. Then they sold him. Joseph's brothers sold him into slavery.

As a slave, Joseph worked diligently and received favor. He still believed in the dream that God had placed on his heart. He was not going to let something small (hah!) like being sold into slavery stop him.

Eventually he would achieve a position of influence as the chief slave in the home of Potiphar, a prominent Egyptian leader at the time. Potiphar's wife was naughty though. And one time when her king was away, the wife came out to play. She lunged at Joseph, wanting to engage him sexually. Joseph, true to his convictions, declined the invitation, and at the wrong moment, he was caught in an innocent but compromising scene. Not wanting her husband to perceive her as guilty, Potiphar's wife accused Joseph of rape, and Potiphar threw him into prison. Once again, while in prison, Joseph gradually gained more influence.

He worked his way up to chief prisoner—not a title I would be happy with if I were him. He made friends with the guards and the other prisoners and interpreted their dreams there, a move that would eventually bring his own dream to fruition.

Pharaoh began to have dreams and tried everything to understand what they meant. After Pharoah had tried just about everything he could think of, one of Joseph's old prison buddies spoke up about the dreamer. And at just the right time, God brought everything together.

Joseph was able to interpret the dreams Pharaoh was having. This move positioned him to set up the nation well for hard times that were to come. Pharaoh also placed Joseph in a prominent position as the second in command over their country. Some years later and just like he dreamed, Joseph's brothers came to Egypt needing food and bowed to their younger brother, though not realizing it was he. Joseph later revealed himself, showing grace and mercy to his brothers.

This is a pretty familiar story in the Bible, but let's unpack it together as it lays out a great foundation to how we can achieve dreams.

the theme of your heart

From the very first moment that Joseph had a dream about carrying the weight of influence, he was diligent to keep that marker as the theme of his heart. That central position of acknowledgment allowed him to continuously work toward influential positions regardless of whether it was as a slave, prisoner, or national hero.

He shared his dreams with others unashamedly but did not boast about them. By walking in a confidence he gained by what he felt God revealed to him, Joseph was able to withstand any criticism or false accusation that came along.

Something becoming the theme of your heart does not happen overnight. You have to allow the promises of God to take root inside you. As you meditate on God's Word, passion for the things of the Lord will grow deeper inside you. Pieces of the chaos that exist in the world will begin to drift away, and your heart will set itself solely on God's dream for your life.

Since that moment when I was ten years old and the school counselor unknowingly prophesied over me, my heart's theme has been to be a messenger of the gospel. Quite literally, I began having dreams at night of standing on stages in churches, arenas, and stadiums declaring the truth of Jesus. Our dreams at night are one of the ways God breathes into us our destiny.

By the time I got to college, some of life's challenges had squeezed their way into my heart. I lost focus of God's call on my life. I began preaching when I was a freshman in high school. God had used me all over my region to preach in dozens of churches. But I took a break when I departed for Missouri State University.

I was considering what my career should be. I was majoring in public relations with a minor in ethical leadership. My professor Mrs. Kyle brought in several guest speakers to help us understand different possible career paths. One was a Missouri State alumnus who went to law school and became a government lobbyist. I was inspired and started to think about entering politics again. I looked into law schools and started mapping out a plan to become the youngest governor in Missouri history.

Times of worship and prayer were important to me. In my one-bedroom apartment in Springfield, Missouri, where I went to college, I would routinely turn on a YouTube video of the latest worship songs. One song in particular really spoke to me. It was called "Your Love Never Fails," sung by Chris Quilala of Jesus Culture. I played it on repeat almost every day.

With the lyrics blaring through my iMac, I rested in God's presence while spreading out on a lumpy, red beanbag chair in my living room. This time something happened that I had never experienced before. It felt like Jesus himself had walked into the room.

The Holy Spirit rushed over me, and I felt a tremendous yet gentle weight of supernatural love. My heart longed to feel love like this. It was a surge of supernatural proportions, much like what Lydia experienced in Acts 16. I wanted the feeling to last forever, but I knew it wouldn't. However, it did reawaken me to the calling over my life. At that moment, with that song, the Holy Spirit permanently changed my trajectory.

A few days later, someone offered me a summer internship in youth ministry. I excitedly said yes and never looked back. My political aspirations subsided because I encountered the desires of my heart that were woven into the fabric of my DNA by the Creator.

when no one is watching

I sometimes think about what was going through Joseph's mind as he was sitting in the hole his brothers had thrown him into. I bet he prayed and asked for strength to persevere, that he may achieve what God had called him to.

And again, what was going through his mind as he was stripped naked and sold into slavery? For him to gain influence and positional authority, he had to know that what he did in the small moments would create the future God had planned for him. So he served and refused to cross any boundaries that would negatively affect his integrity.

Then prison. That had to be the hardest place to be sold out to God's promises. Most people in this prison were likely legitimate criminals. They probably did not suddenly become saints once they were locked up. It is really hard to remain faithful when those around you lack character. But Joseph did it, and God honored him for it.

His faithfulness in the small moments built up a trust reservoir with God. God knew that when Joseph ascended to a place of influence, he would handle it exactly the way he was meant to. These moments of refinement built his character so that he led with grace. His small moments of trusting God in the hole, in slavery, and in prison led to the fulfillment of his life's dream. We are what we repeatedly do. Because he learned to trust God when it seemed like his dream was over and no one was watching, one day Joseph was in front of everyone, on the main stage, and God trusted him with an entire nation's survival.

What things are you doing in your life to remain faithful to a dream that God has placed in your heart? How are you building up a trust reservoir with God? Jesus says that those who can be trusted with the small things will be trusted with more. Be faithful when no one is watching and allow the habits of God's lordship over your life to blossom into influence on those around you.

what you want most

Joseph was a young guy who most likely desired a relationship with a woman. And since Potiphar was a prominent leader of the time, his wife had to be attractive and appealing. The thought surely crossed Joseph's mind, even if only for a fraction of a second, that he desired Potiphar's wife. More than he wanted Potiphar's wife, though, he wanted the dream that God placed on his life to come to realization.

When he sat at the pinnacle of his influence, in this scene he had dreamed about, his brothers came and bowed before him in need of food. A lesser man would have banished the brothers from his presence. Joseph had the authority and the right to do the same, but he chose what he wanted most: restoration with his family. He chose to extend grace and lead with what God had given him to do. He and his family returned to a right relationship with each other.

Our culture today is a microwave society in which *now* is easy. *Now* is that extra piece of cake or that new pair of shoes. It's saying what is on our mind and justifying ourselves as we compromise our values. We feel *now* instantly.

Most is hard. *Most* is letting your mouth water unsatisfied or rocking your shoes till the soles fall off. It's being quick to listen and slow to speak and loving others even if they do not deserve it. *Most* takes patience. Haven't you heard it said, "Lost the battle but won the war?" To stay on course for the dream that God has placed in your life, you will fight many now-most battles. Discipline yourself to want *most*. Big dreams take big sacrifices.

lifeplan

At a particularly challenging time in my life, I had surrounded myself with leaders who did not value the gifts God had entrusted to me. Instead, they took advantage of my skills for their personal agendas. It took me some time to realize what had happened. When I did, I felt confused and distracted. Despite what I had been through, I knew God was still calling me to share the gospel, write books, teach online courses, speak at conferences, and lead churches. It was a time when the dream was still in my heart, but the difficulty of the hole, slavery, or prison began to sink in.

Then God connected me to some really great mentors. One of my mentors, Bart, is certified in something called LifePlan. It is a Christ-centered process to help bring focus and clarity to various domains in your life. He offered to help create a LifePlan for me. I accepted, and I spent a few days with him at his house in Las Vegas.

During this process Bart asked me two questions that changed my perspective forever: "At your funeral, what do you want them to remember you for? What is your contribution going to be?" These questions were less about legacy and much more about fulfilling what I believe God wants me to do.

I answered him by saying, "In the end, I want my contribution to be a movement that spreads the aroma of Christ because I have had an intimate relationship with God and have taught people to want to be better." Bart helped me come up with a plan to accomplish this by leaning into the next five years and dreaming what might be possible. I dreamed of writing this book years before I typed a word. It's part of the contribution I feel God wants me to make for the kingdom. I also knew God would position me to help churches and leaders dream big dreams for their ministries and lives.

The dream I believe God has for my life has become my theme; this conversation was a great reminder. It is vital to reframe your perspective so you can continue to operate toward the dream or the position of influence God has for you. In everyone's life there will be moments when we hold the influence of those around us. It could be at work, with our family, or with our peers. When those moments come, how do you want to respond?

Maybe the best questions you can ask yourself today are these: At your funeral, what do you want them to remember you for? What is your contribution going to be?

CHAPTER 2

a new mind

Sometimes I feel scared.

Most of the time when I feel that way, I have no idea what I am afraid of. It comes in waves, gripping me—it's almost paralyzing. I try to do things but can't. I try to think, but my thoughts are stuck, and I'm not really sure why.

Maybe my thoughts are stuck on the absolute worst-case scenarios of my current realities. Usually, the truth about my current reality is that there is far more good than bad, so it's confusing. You see, I have a habit of taking well-calculated risks that tend to be successful. But still I freeze. And I'm still afraid. My biggest enemy is me.

Our negative thoughts and fears can take control of our dreams.

I used to think that the circumstances of someone's life or upbringing were the most important determining factors for their life's outcome. I have since changed my stance on that. I know twin brothers who live drastically different lives. They had the same tough upbringing in the same dysfunctional family. Despite being twins, sharing the same parents, and receiving the same educational opportunities, they ended up on opposite ends of the spectrum. One completed a professional postgraduate degree and is a very successful entrepreneur. The other started community college but didn't finish, can't seem to hold a steady job, and has addiction issues.

My conclusion is that the situation does not determine who you are; rather, it reveals you to yourself. And when you're revealed to yourself, you have choices to make. In this present moment, whatever situation you find yourself in, whether good or bad, it is up to you to continue on the same path or make a change.

Sometimes I get scared. I often have these freeze-up moments. There have been times when I froze and was unable to do what I had set out to do. More often than not, once I learned how to deal with this, I was able to regenerate the fear I felt into positive energy.

The Bible talks about this. It says we have the power to be renewed by our mind. "Do not be conformed to this world, but be transformed by the renewal of your mind, that by testing you may discern what is the will of God, what is good and acceptable and perfect" (Romans 12:2 ESV).

Some of the most successful people I know are the ones who found themselves in the worst of circumstances yet were determined to act and do the work necessary to create a positive outcome. My friend Brian is a great example.

Everyone loves to be around Brian. He's in the life-saving business. For pay, he is a firefighter in his community, but his heart is with his local church. He and his wife have served as youth pastors there for many years. Brian met Dusty while they were both still in high school. Before she was sixteen, they had their first kid and were married. Marrying so young and having a child put a strain not only on their own relationship but also on their relationships with others. The military became a quick fix for Brian, but it did not resolve the issues lingering in his heart. Soon came alcohol. Next, unwise and unfaithful choices that would strain his family even more.

In his lowest moment, alone at his house, Brian held a gun to his head and whispered a single prayer: "God save me if you have a plan for me still." That isolated plea, uttered in one breath, was all God wanted to hear to bring Brian back to life and reveal God's purpose for him. Brian's friend was in the neighborhood and, on a whim, decided to stop by. The perfect timing of the knock on the door startled Brian, and he put down the gun to answer the door. He has never been the same since, almost like the door he opened revealed God instead of his friend.

Every day Brian is forced to deal with the thoughts that once controlled him. Every day, Brian decides that, through Christ, he is more than a conqueror, so he makes a choice to be better. The baby Brian and Dusty had when they were teens is now a college student studying to be a doctor. They have three more kids, too, all adopted from pretty desperate situations. Brian is teaching them what it means to renew their minds every day.

The best way I have learned to renew your mind is through memorizing Scripture. Every time an ungodly thought attacks me, I take it captive and replace it with a promise from God. For example, I got an incurable disease from COVID-19, which has affected many of my daily rhythms. Sometimes I get discouraged and find my inner self saying things like *God must be punishing me* or *I'll never be better*. Instantly, I take control of these thoughts and refuse to allow them ground to grow. I say out loud, "Thank you, Jesus, for being my healer" or "I love you, Jesus." I replace something that clearly is not from God with something that I know is from him.

radical honesty

As the circumstances of life reveal our true selves, the choices we make become internal. It is within ourselves that we make the decision to grow or remain unchanged. It is within ourselves, with the power of the Holy Spirit, that we allow God to renew our minds.

The first and most practical step of this process is radical honesty. Radical honesty is the willingness to accept and admit the truth that God has revealed to you about yourself. To understand how to get to radical honesty, we must first realize that we have a natural propensity to hide from the truth. It's in our gene pool.

we hide

It all started with Adam and Eve.

The world began as a strictly beautiful place, meaning that everything was beautiful and nothing bad or harmful existed. Adam and Eve's willing disobedience of a single rule caused the demise of all mankind. As they both ate from the forbidden tree, Adam and Eve were instilled with the knowledge of good and evil. It was much more of a curse than it sounds, and they immediately recognized the error of their ways. Suddenly, they realized that they were naked and hid their bodies. They heard the Lord walking through the beautiful garden and hid from him.

God, already knowing what they had done, then implanted certain hardships into every human thereafter. This means you and me. We have inherited a gene pool that, literally, since the first humans, includes the tendency to hide.

So I can't help but think that when we are forced to face the truth, our first and natural tendency is to do the same thing Adam and Eve did: we hide from it. Think about it. When you were a kid and your parents caught you doing something you shouldn't be doing for the first time, what did you do? Lie about it? Cover it up? If you didn't, you weren't born on this planet.

As we progress from being a child and enter adolescence and adulthood, we mostly eliminate that behavior, at least externally. Our relationships with those with whom we interact every day largely bend toward honesty because we have learned and adopted that behavior. Most likely, we have learned to be honest from doing the opposite and getting caught. We know there are negative consequences for hiding from the truth. Many people adopt honest behavior externally because that's what they've been taught to do, yet they have not learned how to react with honesty internally.

God covers us

What I love about the story of Adam and Eve is that the covering they created for themselves was insufficient. When they realized they were naked, they took fig leaves and sewed them together with vines or whatever they had available to use. Yes, they were covered, but I am sure the fig leaves left little to the imagination.

They hid from God, but there is really no hiding from God. As Adam and Eve came out from their hiding place, God first delivered a punishment for their sin. What he did next illustrates exactly what could happen to us internally if we choose to seek the Lord rather than hide. God created for them clothing out of animal hide—a fabric, by the way, that is still in use today. The fig-leaf clothing they had designed did not have the strength to stand up against the storms that would come. Animal hide would cover and provide protection.

In life, we can often recognize only glimpses of our true selves. When we choose to deal only with that glimpse of ourselves, we are wearing fig leaves instead of clothing made from hides. When we allow God to be at the center of renewing our mind, he covers us completely. We can withstand the storms that may come. We know that, for Adam and Eve, the truth came with consequences. But now we know that the radical honesty that came from God for Adam and Eve also brought covering and protection beyond what they could provide for themselves.

find someone you trust

Being radically honest can be hard. Since I believe honesty is a learned behavior, I find it helpful to have someone I know who loves me and whom I can trust to help me through this process.

I had a pastor who recognized the freeze-up moments that I would experience. These moments were really embarrassing. What I couldn't admit was that they were prevalent in meetings and gatherings with other people. It turns out they are a symptom of some trauma I experienced growing up, and it took someone whom I trusted to help me work through it and be honest with myself. I knew what was happening to me internally when I froze up, but I would have never admitted it out loud because it's easier to pretend like it doesn't happen—to hide from it (fig leaves!). I could actually fool myself into thinking that no one realized what was going on but me.

When my pastor confronted me about these episodes, I was embarrassed and played the fool (denial). But, after sensing he was truly on my side and really trying to help me, I felt much better about being open and honest with him. We were able to find the root of the problem in that trauma I had experienced when I was younger.

Just because I was honest and open with him, and we found the root of my problem, does not mean the problem disappeared. I was forced to face and decide which option I would choose, something that continues to this very day. My mind had to be renewed. It was very difficult at first. I learned that the more honest I was, the more covering and protection God gave me in the form of strength.

When Nathan confronted King David about his sin with Bathsheba, David had been keeping that affair a secret for quite some time. The bond Nathan and King David shared enabled David to bring out and deal with this struggle. David was able to confide in Nathan, whom he trusted, and remained king because the Lord was able to provide healing.

Like King David, when I came out of hiding with someone whom I trusted, the Lord provided healing.

courageous decision-making

The next step to having a new mind is courageous decision-making.

Victims have overtaken our culture. Many people refuse to take responsibility for themselves and instead delight in the false sense of security that comes with blaming others for their own troubles. What many of these victim-minded people do not realize is that taking responsibility allows them to heal. It takes courageous decision-making to experience that healing. The turmoil and circumstances in which some people live are of their own making. These include those who cheated on their spouse, could not control their spending, or have an untamed tongue.

Others have been touched by evil and forced to live in situations they did not create. People have abused them, abandoned them, or taken advantage of them, or they were simply in the wrong place at the wrong time. The route to any of these circumstances is vastly different, but the way out can be the same.

created turmoil

The Bible describes Peter as someone who created his own turmoil. Peter was one of Jesus' closest friends—one of the top three to be exact. Jesus actually said he was going to use Peter to build his church. Yet, just before Jesus died on the cross, Peter denied even knowing him. The Bible goes on to tell us that this happened three times before the sun had even risen. Imagine how Peter felt! After being by Jesus' side nonstop for three years, Peter denied knowing him on the very same day that Jesus died. The Bible says Peter wept bitterly over this moment.

Judas is another example of someone who created his own circumstance. Judas was one of the twelve disciples with Jesus during his span of ministry. When the opportunity arose to turn Jesus over to the authorities who were seeking him, Judas turned his back on his Savior and gave him up for a few dollars.

You and I have encountered situations that have created turmoil in our lives. Some situations may be big, and others may be small. The path to healing resides within these moments but only if we learn our lessons well. Few differences exist between the choices Peter and Judas made. There is, however, an enormous difference in their responses afterward.

When forced to deal with the reality of what he had done, Peter came back. He did not run away. In the gospel of Mark, when Jesus rose from the tomb, the angel mentioned only Peter by name along with the other unnamed disciples. The first disciple Jesus wanted to see after conquering death was his good friend Peter. Peter made the decision to put aside his grief and shame and see Jesus.

It takes courage to show up when you know the circumstance hasn't been good. Peter grieved his mistakes and chose to rise above them. Judas, unwilling to accept the redemptive work of the cross, disengaged by hanging himself. I am certain that Jesus would have forgiven Judas if he had chosen the path Peter took.

touched by evil

I encountered evil in the form of childhood trauma that created these freeze-up moments in my life. Really, I was stuck in it and had not learned to get past my past. In many ways, I played a victim internally. I was able to make courageous decisions when I chose to be radically honest with others and God and take action by correcting some of my weaknesses.

Like me, my friend Lexie is someone who encountered trauma through no fault of her own. When she was just a kid, someone she trusted sexually abused her in the basement of her own home. As if that wasn't enough, when she was twelve, her neighbor began to exploit her. He was older and told her that he loved her. She was a child and didn't know any different. She thought she loved him. Her neighbor told her that when certain cars were at his house, she was to ride her bike to his house on a special route that he mapped out. When she got there, he drugged her and sold her to other men for short-term sessions of hell on earth. This went on until she reached puberty and the pedophiles were no longer interested in her.

Years went by before Lexie realized that she had been sex-trafficked out of her own house. She was in college and found in a textbook a definition that described her experience. She knew the baggage she carried because of what these men had done and finally came to grips with it.

Now as a young adult, Lexie is a nationally known activist fighting for young girls throughout the country who find themselves in similar circumstances. She had a reality TV show on A&E, speaks at many conferences, trains hundreds of law enforcement personnel in recognizing and dealing with sex trafficking, and even holds press conferences about the topic, once with the governor of New Jersey at the Super Bowl.[1]

Lexie could have walked away from ever experiencing love again. She could have felt worthless for the rest of her life. She could have played the victim card to gain sympathy from those around her. But like Peter, she chose to act, beginning with radical honesty about her situation and taking steps to deal with it.

action required

Entitlement arises from being given excessive gifts without any regard for the cost or value of the gift. Without understanding the cost, you have no idea how to properly steward and attain the gift again. True luxury comes from having an excess of what you earned through your journey with God because you know how to get it again.

I can't help but think that many of the bad situations we find ourselves in are opportunities to gain the strength of a new mind. The process of gaining a renewed mind will instill immeasurable value. The inheritance that we receive due to the sins of Adam and Eve requires reprogramming our brain. We should see this as a gift more than anything else. We have seen the behavior of entitlement Adam and Eve displayed when they did not properly understand how to steward the gift of their beautiful lives. Now we have the opportunity to see the difference God can make by restoring our post-fall minds into something beautiful once we turn to him. Simply put, we must have a resolve to keep going when we feel like quitting. Peter kept going. Lexie kept going. Brian kept going. I keep going.

Judas quit.

The Holy Spirit is working within you. Keep going. Don't give up. The power from him makes you more than a conqueror. In the Bible, 1 Corinthians 9:24–26 says to run the race that is before us with our eyes on the prize that is eternal and to not give up.

David Schultz was a wrestler for the United States Olympics wrestling team. He won a gold medal! One of his friends told me that when asked about his achievements and what it takes to be the best wrestler in the world, David replied that his motivation is simple: keep trying. He explained that when the first period is over, some wrestlers say, "I'm going to give all I have this next period." Great wrestlers give everything they have each minute. When the first minute is up, they say, "I'm going to give all I have this next minute." But the world's best wrestler gives everything that he has every second. When the first second is up, David said, "I'm going to give all that I have this next second." And when that second is up, he said, "I'm going to give all that I have this next second."

What would it look like for you to give all that you have each second to achieve renewal by the power of the cross?

List some areas where you have compromised your end goals by seeking immediate satisfaction. For example, I have a friend who desires financial freedom but uses shopping as an escape mechanism. What are some things you may need to give up to step into a fully renewed mind?

CHAPTER 3

i once was blind

Have you ever been blind? Or maybe you've suffered an eye injury, experienced a temporary loss of sight, or had to undergo vision surgery. When was the last time you couldn't see? Maybe you just have trouble seeing sometimes. You might wear glasses, bifocals, or contact lenses. But if you're reading this with your own eyes, you're probably not completely blind.

The World Health Organization estimates that worldwide, at least 2.2 billion people suffer some sort of vision impairment.[2] That's over 27 percent of the world's population.

But 100 percent of the population is born blind. Not physically but spiritually.

So let me ask you again: When was the last time you couldn't see?

all i know

Jesus was walking through a village one day when he met a young man who had been blind since birth. The man was begging, which was the only thing a blind person could do for a living in those days. And Jesus had compassion on him in the most unique way. Jesus spit on the ground, bent over, and stirred the spit into the dirt. He then formed some mud and scooped it up. He called the man over and smeared the mud on the man's eyes. Then Jesus told the man to go wash his face in the pool of Siloam. Instantly the man could see!

But Jesus faced some opposition. You see, this all took place on a Saturday, or the Sabbath day. That is the day when the law requires all Jews to rest from work. What kind of work? All kinds of work. That includes working in the field and working in the house. It includes tilling your land and harvesting your grain. And it even includes making mud. That little act of spitting on the ground, mixing up the dirt, and spreading it on the man's face was considered work. And the Pharisees, the ones who liked to guard the law and make sure everyone obeyed it to the letter, were not happy about it.

Instead of going after Jesus, though, they decided to put the beggar on trial. A man who just regained his sight. A man whose only crime was being healed. They accused him of being a sinner, then they accused Jesus of being a sinner. But I love this man's response: "I know this: I was blind, and now I can see!" (John 9:25).

I can relate. I've been blind before. And now I can see. I'm not talking about physical blindness. I'm talking about the type of blindness that holds us all back, keeps us from moving forward, and can freeze us in place.

Being resilient in our faith is all about finding the steps to move forward. The problem is we start out groping in the darkness. We don't know the first move to make, and we can't even see to make that move. I've been there, and I think maybe you have too. And I want to help you take the first step.

amazing grace

In any survey of the most recognizable hymns, "Amazing Grace" is usually at the top. If you grew up in church, I imagine you have the words memorized. Those of you who were really committed probably know all four verses by heart. Perhaps the most memorable part of that song is in the final refrain of the first verse: "I once…was blind, but now I see." Recovery of sight for the man born blind is one of the most incredible miracles we read about in Scripture. Yet all of us have the opportunity to go from blind to seeing.

"Amazing Grace" was written by an Anglican clergyman, John Newton. That probably doesn't surprise you at all. It makes sense that a minister would write a song about God's great grace for his people. What you may not know is that John Newton had a personal reason to write that song.

Born in London in 1725 to a sailor father, young John Newton found himself on ships pretty early in life. At only eighteen, he was visiting friends overseas when he was captured by some British sailors and forced to join the Royal Navy. He hated it. He tried to desert the ship but was caught and punished. In front of the rest of the crew, he was stripped to his waist and beaten while tied to the main mast.

Humiliated and still fuming at his commanding officer, he asked for a transfer to a slave ship. The crew would sail to Africa and exchange goods for enslaved people, whom the ship then carried to the Caribbean and the American colonies. But the lucrative slave trade still left Newton empty.

At the age of twenty, his fellow crew members abandoned him in West Africa, where he found himself enslaved. After three long years of constant ridicule, hard labor, and even beatings, fellow Englishmen rescued Newton, and he was finally sent home. It was during that voyage that he gave his heart to Jesus. During a violent storm at sea, he called out to God for help. The boat did not sink. He was saved! In more ways than one.

But he didn't give up slave trading. He still helped others buy and sell human beings, shipping men and women far away from their families in exchange for money. It was the only life he knew, but he was about to find a new one.

After a stroke stopped him from sailing, Newton had a short career as a tax collector, of all things. During that time, he studied the Bible and traveled to churches to preach. He was soon ordained in the Anglican Church. In 1779, he worked together with a musician to pen his most famous hymn, "Amazing Grace." Nearly ten years later, he finally took up the cause of abolition, preaching against the slave trade that was once his source of fortune.[3] He once was blind—blinded by his situation in life. He was nearly bought and sold like the enslaved people he, too, bought and sold. He could not see that God was moving behind the scenes of his life.

He once was blind—blinded by his own self-image. Feeling he was only good for sea work or slave trading, he couldn't truly realize what God had in store for him.

He once was blind—blinded by his own idea of who God was. How could a man have such an incredible conversion experience and then spend nearly a decade in the slave business? It was because he didn't fully understand who it was who had saved him.

He once was blind—but then he saw clearly. And it was in that moment that he truly came alive.

what's holding you back?

We must clear our own blindness if we ever hope to move forward. I want to help you clear your blindness and get a new sense of resilience in your life. Let's start by imagining a better world, one where we know what we want, what we were made for, and who is leading us. Just think how great your life could be! Think how many people you could impact for the kingdom of God. How much meaning each day would have. All those things are possible if you will only take the first step and keep moving.

The first hurdle you need to overcome is the situation you're in right now. We all live in situations beyond our control and circumstances resulting from our poor decisions. We are surrounded by a broken world that causes us grief and pain. We are overcome by this sorry, sinful state. But that doesn't mean that we have to stay there. We all have struggles, failures, and sin. How we deal with them will determine if and when we can move forward.

We need to take a fresh look at our situation in life. We must get a clear view of what's really going on. Instead of seeing only struggles, we must see our situation as an instrument to strengthen us to make another move. Instead of focusing on failure, we must see opportunities around every corner. Instead of wallowing in our sins, we must confess them and move on in repentance.

There was a season in my life when I was afraid to confess my sin to God. It was like I wasn't sure if he would still accept me. I would go through two to three days of thinking about my sin, even feeling nervous about my mistakes. If I committed a big sin on a Friday night, I would skip church on Sunday. A Joyce Meyer sermon was the catalyst for me. I remember her saying, "When should you repent? *Immediately!*" No one had taught me you could do that. It has become my practice now.

"There is no condemnation for those who belong to Christ Jesus" (Romans 8:1). In other words, when we enter a relationship with Jesus, we are righteous. Shame and condemnation are not from God. They are tactics from the Enemy to stall us on our way to our destiny. If the Enemy can get us isolated, we will be too intimidated to work on our blind spots, thus never being propelled toward our calling.

The next hurdle we must overcome to become more resilient is our self-image. We all have a desire to do something great. Why not let God do that within us and watch him work it out of us? Instead of self-doubt, see the greatness of the dream God has given you. And then you need to find new ways to gain insight.

Grab hold of the dream God put in you. He created you and cares for you. He wants to see you do great things. But first, you must identify the blind spots in your life. Like a log in your eye, they can hinder your movement. Clear them out, and then you can activate your strengths and become all that God intended for you to be.

The last hurdle we clear as we become more resilient is how we see God. Imagining our Lord can be a tricky thing. Our lives, our influences, what we read and watch on TV, whom we interact with, and how we view ourselves often will give us a wrong picture of who God is. Without a clear vision of him, we will be left wondering how to move forward.

Instead of a genie in the sky or a disappointed dad, he is a God who sees you and wants you to see. He is a God who bankrupted heaven so that you could have a future. He is a God who never leaves you or forsakes you even when you feel all alone and abandoned. And he is a God moving behind the scenes to orchestrate the greatest possible future for you.

The best way to motivate you to movement is to find out who God is to those who are in a relationship with him. When you realize he wants to be your friend first and foremost, you can't wait to spend time with him, enter his rest, and enjoy his grace. If you don't already know him, my prayer is that by the time you finish reading this book, you will meet him and start a new stage of your own life. My prayer is that we never again get stuck. I hope that these words will inspire dreams, prompt action, and keep momentum firing as you learn what you never knew about your world, yourself, and your God.

light at the end of the tunnel

When you finally get that new sight, that clear vision, going from blind to seeing fully, it's like waking up. It's like a brand-new day. It's like that new life we all long for.

I know what it feels like because I've experienced it. And I want you to experience it too. I want you to live a more resilient life, one where you can be more confident about your decisions. A life where you know who you are, why you're here, and where you're going. A life that you live for the glory of God, not your own glory.

That life is just ahead. It may feel dark right now. It may be hard to see. But just ahead is a light, like the light at the end of the tunnel. Are you ready for what's on the other side? Are you ready to see your situation in a brand-new light, where struggles and failures no longer hold you back? Are you ready to see yourself in a brand-new light, where you are clearing blind spots and activating your strengths? Are you ready to see God in a brand-new light, where he is who he says he is and does what he says he will do?

I wasn't ready at first. I held on to my heartache and pain like a loyal friend. But once I took the plunge and embraced my destiny in Christ, it was almost like the Tyler Feller I once was had passed away and a new me came to life right then.

Your journey can begin today. I'm not going to promise you it will be quick. It will take some hard work, some self-evaluation, some early mornings or late nights. You may want to give up and go back. But I want you to know that it will be worth all the work you put into it. I can guarantee you a return on this investment. Because it's not my promise but God's promise.

David's soul-searching prayer is one of my favorites:

> Search me, O God, and know my heart;
> test me and know my anxious thoughts.

Point out anything in me that offends you,
and lead me along the path of everlasting life.
(Psalm 139:23–24)

Before you get into the next chapter, spend a few minutes with the Holy Spirit. Pray this: *God, is there anything in my heart that needs to be brought to the light? Please search me, God. Do I have any blind spots? Point out anything that offends you. Purge from me anything that's not of you.*

Write some notes on what God reveals to you.

PART TWO

the truth about your situation

When we learn the truth about our situation, we can go from stuck to striving, from frozen to flourishing. We finally see our struggles and failures as opportunities. And we rest assured that God is on our side, helping us every step of the way.

CHAPTER 4

the struggle is real

"That's easy for you to say!"

Have you ever had that thrown in your face? I know I have. Because I'm a pastor, people sort of assume that it's easy for me to follow my own advice. When I talk about praying and reading the Bible daily, I hear, "That's easy for you because it's your job." Or when I talk about keeping yourself pure from sin, I hear, "Well, it's easy for you since you're a pastor and all."

I want you to know it's not easy. I struggle just like anyone else. With finding time to dig into God's rest. With keeping temptation at bay. And with holding back the urge to just stop in my tracks. To not take one more step. To just give up.

As a pastor, I often find myself convicted from my own sermons. I can easily point out that the text says to give above and beyond, pray daily, fast often, and be a diligent student of the Word. I'm not always great at it personally. I hate to admit it, but there are days when I totally forget to read the Bible. I also preach a lot about demonstrating the fruit of the Spirit. In other words, be patient and kind. I am not always patient or kind.

Whenever someone gives tough advice, the audience looks for an escape or an excuse. We like to think that some people are just special and we're not so that we can go on living the way we have. We have a start-and-stop life, full of hiccups and false beginnings, with no clear victory ahead. *That person over there? They've got it all together. That's why they can give me that advice. But it's advice I can't take. Not me.*

When you look deeper into that person's life, however, you'll find the same struggles that you have every day. And no matter how crazy that advice will sound, there's always a moment in time in that person's life that made those words spring to life. A struggle that birthed that sentiment. Take this verse from the Bible, for instance. I'm going to warn you that it's a bit tough to swallow. You may want to get warmed up before you read it.

Are you ready? Okay, let's try it:

"We can rejoice, too, when we run into problems and trials, for we know that they help us develop endurance" (Romans 5:3).

Wow, okay. That's a tough one. Rejoice in our problems, our trials, and our struggles? Really, Paul? That's easy for you to say. I want to hear these verses instead:

"We can get overwhelmed, too, when we run into problems and trials…"

"We can try to just get through life, too, when we run into problems and trials…"

"We can give up trying, too, when we run into problems and trials…"

Those make a lot more sense, don't they? Those are the messages you probably hear in your head every time you come up against struggles in life. We avoid them at all costs. And when we do encounter them, we either stop dead in our tracks or we turn and retreat.

Paul wants us to rejoice in our problems. Thank God for the joy of facing struggles! Yeah, right. *That's easy for you to say, Paul.* He was an apostle. Called by God. Special. He worked miracles. God healed the sick through him. He received visions from God. You can't tell me his life was just like mine. There's no way he faced struggles too.

Well, I have some news for you. He didn't face the kind of struggles you and I face. He faced worse. Unless your life has been full of prison and beatings and prison beatings. Unless you have been lost in the woods without a guide or kept in the cold without a coat. Unless you've been shipwrecked and adrift at sea, starved, beaten, and worked to exhaustion, then your struggles may be pretty minor compared to Paul's (2 Corinthians 11:23–27).

Paul lived a hard life. And he never gave up. That's what is so inspiring about his story and also so convicting about his words. When I read that he told us to rejoice in struggles and I see the number of struggles he faced, I know I get a bit choked up.

All right, Paul. I'll buy into this idea.

My dysfunctional upbringing embedded into my psyche the idea that bad days are more common than good days. Sometimes I would wake up in a terrible mood and live with the expectation that nothing good was possible over the next twenty-four hours. The Holy Spirit convicted me of this attitude. God reminded me that we are supposed to rejoice in each day and be glad for it. I wrote on a small whiteboard on my refrigerator, "Rejoice! Today is the day the Lord has made, and he only makes good things. Therefore, today is going to be a good day!" It was a daily prophetic declaration.

I repeated these words thousands of times across hundreds of days. God used them to rewire my brain and, over time, completely change my expectations. Now it's rare that I wake up in a bad mood. It's even rarer for me not to believe it's going to be a great day. I learned to rejoice in my struggles. I created a list of ten prophetic declarations I say over my life almost every day now, placing into practice the instruction from Paul.

what's stopping you?

I want to ask you a serious question. And be honest with me about it. Actually, be honest with yourself. What in your life is stopping you from being exactly who God wants you to be?

Many of us are stuck in life, failing to make it through the day without wanting to throw in the towel. Some of us self-sabotage, looking for ways to cut our losses and just leave. And then there are those out there who find it hard to get out of bed, put one foot in front of the other, and move forward in life. My heart aches for every one of you who feels that way. I've been there, and I never want to go back. I don't want you to spend another moment stuck in that same way.

For many of us, it's not what's inside us but what's outside that has kept us from moving. It may be situations we have put ourselves into. It could be mounting debt that won't go away when we really want to start a new business venture. It may be a habit or addiction that keeps tripping us up. Or it could be a bad relationship that leaves us feeling regretful. It may be a circumstance, something outside our control. Something bad happened to you, or worse, someone did something bad to you. You were hurt, wounded, damaged. You've been left broken, weak, scarred. But because it happened *to* you instead of *by* you, you feel powerless to make any change, make any difference, gain any resilience in life.

These are the root struggles of many people. What are yours? That's where you need to begin, by identifying that struggle, the thing that keeps you from moving forward with confidence. Name it.

You might struggle with work or school, family or friendships. It might be a struggle with self-image or self-doubt. Whatever that struggle is, it's never too big to stop you if you have God on your side. There is reason to rejoice, even in our struggles.

What's our immediate response to a struggle? Some of us bear down and just endure it. For others, a struggle completely sidetracks us. For most of us, it gives us a reason to stop moving forward. When I think about some of the dysfunction I grew up in, I realize that those patterns followed me into my young adulthood. As a child, my strategy to escape chaos was to hide in my room. Not a bad strategy for an eleven-year-old. Not the wisest thing to do as a twenty-two-year-old professional. I have learned that you can't pretend problems don't exist.

Paul doesn't say to ignore the struggle. He says to rejoice in the struggle because it produces endurance and resilience. That means your struggle can actually produce the opposite of its intended effect. Instead of stopping you, it can make you stronger.

Struggles are real. There's no use closing your eyes, ignoring them, or wishing them away. They won't leave you alone. Your situations and circumstances are part of you. It's how you respond that will determine how far you will go.

So what's stopping you? Really, what's holding you back and keeping you from God's best for your life? Put a name on it. Maybe even write it down. Now let's try to see how switching our perspective on that thing will help us keep going.

paul: the anti-instagrammer

Do you know what Instagram syndrome is? It's when you see someone's life through the carefully curated lens of social media and think that's really how they are. Filtered for full effect, their pictures tell a story different from reality. They edit out all the negative circumstances or harmful situations to show you a made-up world.

Don't worry. We all do it. But Paul didn't. If he had Instagram back then, his posts would rock your world because he never sugarcoated any part of his life. He told it like it is. Just take a look at one paragraph that seems to sum up Paul's life:

> I have worked harder, been put in prison more often, been whipped times without number, and faced death again and again. Five different times the Jewish leaders gave me thirty-nine lashes. Three times I was beaten with rods. Once I was stoned. Three times I was shipwrecked. Once I spent a whole night and a day adrift at sea. I have traveled on many long journeys. I have faced danger from rivers and from robbers. I have faced danger from my own people, the Jews, as well as from the Gentiles. I have faced danger in the cities, in the deserts, and on the seas. And I have faced danger from men who claim to be believers but are not. I have worked hard and long, enduring many sleepless nights. I have been hungry and thirsty and have often gone without food. I have shivered in the cold, without enough clothing to keep me warm. (2 Corinthians 11:23–27)

Wow! Just imagine that on your Facebook bio. I don't know how many of us would click on your stories, but they would definitely be…interesting. But Paul's stories were captured not by social media but by his traveling companion, Luke, and he put them down on paper in a book called Acts. Those shipwrecks Paul talked about? Luke wrote about one of them in Acts 27. And that story is a perfect example of why we need to keep rejoicing through the struggles.

Let me set it up for you. Roman soldiers arrested Paul in Jerusalem for basically starting a riot in the temple. They were about to beat him, but then he revealed that he was a Roman citizen. Citizenship gave him certain rights, like not being bludgeoned to death without a fair trial. Plus, as a Roman citizen, he could ask that the trial be in front of Caesar.

The Romans gave in and put him on a ship headed for Rome. It was a journey they had taken a thousand times, but this time it was going to go all wrong. "Putting out to sea from there, we encountered strong headwinds that made it difficult to keep the ship on course" (Acts 27:4). So you can see, almost from the start, this trip was not going to be easy.

Some of us are born with the wind in our face. Some of us are born with wind in our sails. But we are all going to have some turbulence at some point in our voyage. It's a great reminder that even under the most divinely authored conditions, Paul faced some of that too.

But that bad headwind was just the start. In verse 8, Luke talked about the struggles and difficulty of the journey. In verse 9, it was the dangerous sea travel. Verse 10 is where he acknowledged that there was "trouble ahead" including loss of cargo, perhaps loss of life, and definitely shipwreck. Was it time to take stock and put an end to this journey? Maybe just slack off a little, come at it with clear eyes later? Nope. It was time to keep moving forward.

what's the worst that could happen?

If you're reading this book, then I'll bet you like books. May I recommend another one? It's called *The Worst-Case Scenario Survival Handbook* by Joshua Piven and David Borgenicht. You can find it online, in bookstores, and probably at your local outdoor outfitter.

This book is great! It teaches you how to survive in the most unmanageable circumstances and situations. No matter what comes your way, this book will prepare you. Alligators attacking? It's got you covered. Stuck in an avalanche? No need to worry. Find yourself in the middle of a military coup in a foreign country while on vacation? Yep, this book has that too! It's a great tool to help you prepare for the most dangerous situations. But it's horrible for dealing with the troubles you face in your day-to-day life.

Let's be honest. You probably won't have to worry about an enemy insurrection during your lunch break. You might never come face-to-face with a worst-case scenario. But so many of us live our lives as if we will. We face a circumstance or situation and think, *What's the worst that can happen?* And then we react to that scenario. We actually live out our lives expecting the worst instead of leaning into God's provision. What happens when we view life through the lens of a worst-case scenario? We think that every small problem is a big hurdle. We believe that every little mess is a huge mistake. It does something to our heart when we view our situations in this warped way. Instead of using *The Worst-Case Scenario Handbook* for our daily struggles, we need to turn to God's handbook, his Word. It's full of promises that he will keep, no matter what.

Back to Paul's story. He was on the boat, and the weather was getting bad. There was an abrupt change in wind direction. The sailors were having trouble turning the ship. Then, suddenly, a storm called a northeaster came sweeping at them like a typhoon! It swept them off course and out to sea. They were in a worst-case scenario, for sure. How did they respond?

First, they got desperate. Fear will lead us to make bad decisions at the worst times. We abandon the things that are actually protecting us. That's what these sailors did. "The next day, as gale-force winds continued to batter the ship, the crew began throwing the cargo overboard. The following day they even took some of the ship's gear and threw it overboard" (Acts 27:18–19). Obviously, they were trying to lighten the load to gain control of the ship. They were facing a struggle and were desperate to try anything just to stay afloat. So they started tossing things overboard.

I think it's interesting that desperation led these sailors to toss provisions. We do that too. We get rid of the habits and disciplines in our lives that are actually making us stronger. When you face a struggle, what is the first thing to get tossed? Maybe you panic and take out a loan to cover the loan you already took out. Maybe you jump ship on a relationship, cutting people out of your life and isolating yourself. Or perhaps what you toss first is the time you should spend with the Lord every day. We get shortsighted when we go to that worst-case scenario. And it can leave us without the real nourishment we need from God.

Next, the sailors lost all hope. They were sapped of strength and fading fast. "The terrible storm raged for many days, blotting out the sun and the stars, until at last all hope was gone" (Acts 27:20). Think about what happens when a struggle hits you out of nowhere. You go from seeing clearly to having cloudy vision. You start to lose sight of God's promises and provisions. And then you lose hope. Your struggles were never meant to take away your hope. Paul learned this lesson and repeated it in Romans 5.

Struggles can build endurance as long as we maintain hope in God. God allows you to struggle to instill courage and power in you so you can get through this trial and then the next one, the next one, the next one, and so on. Struggles can build our faith and give us hope. But when we lose that hope, we start to spiral out of control.

When I was offered an internship as a volunteer youth pastor, I was amazed that someone would trust me to be a leader and Bible teacher. It was my first real opportunity in church leadership. When I met with the pastor and he showed me the ministry space for students, I was incredibly discouraged. Honestly, I began to question if I had just made a dumb decision by signing up for this task. There were so many great ministries that I looked up to. They had state-of-the-art facilities, multiple members of support staff, and years of building a strong foundation.

The ministry space I was given was a glorified storage shed. At most, it fit thirty students. The single computer took more than ten minutes to kick on. The projector was fuzzy and had an orange hue to it. The one light we had in the center of the room hung from the ceiling by a wire. The ceiling was eight feet tall, and teenagers loved jumping to touch it and watch the popcorn-ceiling particles blend in with the stained (and smelly) carpet. The one microphone we used was left over from a PlayStation *Rock Band* game.

Because my mind was stuck comparing this to the ministries I looked up to, it felt like an uphill battle that I wasn't sure I knew how to navigate. I was scared that my first solo ministry venture would be a failure. I'm glad the pastor and church believed in me—but I didn't believe in myself. I almost quit before I started, but I am thankful I decided not to. It was not easy to figure out how to get started. I bought a tank top and a skateboard because I saw some students skating around town. I thought I would hit the streets and get the word out about our new ministry.

There were ten students who attended the ministry when I began. I asked them to dream about what God could do in our ministry if we all gave everything we had to it. We planned for a grand opening service about six weeks later. We met a couple of times per week and prayed, believed, and bounced ideas off each other.

On the day of the ministry launch, students were lined up on the street, wrapping around the block. We were amazed. There were more teenagers than we could count, far beyond what could fit in the room. The pastor and I quickly removed all the chairs from the room, hoping we could squeeze them in without that barrier. It was an incredible night when many students came to know Jesus. Several are serving in ministry leadership today.

The Holy Spirit convicted me that evening. I almost gave up because I was envious of what resources other youth pastors had. This is why Jesus' words in Matthew 10 became one of my favorite passages. "Don't think you have to put on a fund-raising campaign before you start. You don't need a lot of equipment. You are the equipment, and all you need to keep that going is three meals a day. Travel light" (vv. 9–10 MSG).

Sometimes we believe the struggles we face are obstacles when they are quite the opposite. Struggles present opportunities for growth and creative solutions. When we press in instead of giving up, often God shows up in a miraculous way. By leaning into the hard place, you are stepping into the fullness of your capacity and reaching the height of God's plan for your life.

One of my favorite stories from this youth ministry experience happened a few months after the grand opening. Jonah, a seventh-grade student, had an enormous burden for a friend of his at school who declared himself an atheist. Every single week for months, Jonah would ask me to pray with him for this friend. Eventually, I started praying on my own, *God, Jonah has so much faith. You gotta do something!*

Out of the blue one week, that student showed up at our ministry. Since we had gotten rid of all the chairs, he awkwardly sat cross-legged on the carpet while the other students stood and passionately worshiped. He didn't say anything during my sermon and instead just stared at me blankly. It was not going well. However, he showed up again the next week. This time he was much more comfortable and began participating in the same way the other students were. At the end of the night, he decided to follow Jesus. Jonah's prayer was answered! I asked the friend what made him come to our ministry. He said, "I got grounded. As my punishment, my parents made me go to church. They only knew about this church because we drove by a few months ago and saw everyone lined up around the block."

God used our lack of space and equipment as a tool to reach someone who was an atheist. The very struggle that almost caused me to throw in the towel was the one thing God used to make a difference! I have been able to be a part of dozens of stories just like this one over the years.

By the way, Jonah graduated from seminary and pastors a church now too.

divine desperation

What are you going through? What shipwreck do you see just ahead of you? This hardship can either sap you of your strength or instill hope. But how do we make that shift? It takes surrendering to God. Desperation is not necessarily a bad thing. It all depends on where we place our hope. If our hope is in God, a divine desperation, then we know we will never be disappointed. But desperation that we combine with human effort will never see us through.

Paul stood up on the deck of the ship, rain blasting against him. I imagine he had to almost shout over the roar of the wind and waves. And this is what he said: "Take courage! None of you will lose your lives, even though the ship will go down. For last night an angel of the God to whom I belong and whom I serve stood beside me, and he said, 'Don't be afraid, Paul, for you will surely stand trial before Caesar! What's more, God in his goodness has granted safety to everyone sailing with you'" (Acts 27:22–24).

Theologian Willie James Jennings, writing about this passage, said, "The prophetic word always comes at the times when hope is drained, because God will not allow hope to die in this world."[4] Isn't that so reassuring! Paul was desperate for answers. He knew that God had told him he'd see Rome. But how were they going to get out of this mess? He placed that desperate situation in the hands of God.

The struggle you face can never stop the vision God gave you. Why should we ever stop? Why should we ever give up? Let's use all situations and circumstances that try to knock us off course to find renewed energy for the race.

Paul relied on the revelation he received from God. And we have that same revelation right at our fingertips. When we spend time with God in his divine rest, it has to include searching out his Word for answers. Look at how God's Word empowered Paul for the rest of his journey.

First, God's Word came right on time. Right when things were at their worst, Paul reassured the whole crew. It was a timely answer to their current struggle. God will answer you right when you need him if you are consistently seeking him.

Next, God's Word cast out fear. Twice in this speech Paul said to "take courage," and that's because God had already told him not to be afraid. If you constantly live under the threat of a worst-case scenario, you will live in fear. But when you rely on God's Word, there is no room for fear in your life.

Finally, God's Word created a way out. God, in his wisdom, used Paul to come up with a plan for survival. It wasn't the easiest plan. It still took effort. But it was a way out. Here's how Paul braced them for God's plan: "So take courage! For I believe God. It will be just as he said. But we will be shipwrecked on an island" (Acts 27:25–26). Just take a second to realize how encouraging that is. Paul didn't sugarcoat it or tell a lie. He got real with them. This wasn't a made-up Instagram moment. This was the hard truth—"We will be shipwrecked."

You may hit the rocks in life. I'm not going to promise that you won't. But I do know that a God who provides a way out can overcome any shipwreck in your life. Believe in that! Divine desperation means we grab on to God no matter what happens in life. Regardless of the struggle, we move forward, not backward.

the struggle is not the end

God never intended for your struggle to be the end of your story. In many ways, it's just the beginning. This was not the end of Paul's life. It could have been, but it wasn't. He had plenty of struggles ahead. He would be put under house arrest in Rome. He would have to gather a legal team and prepare a defense. He would be without a job, so he would need support. I think this shipwreck was a way for God to prepare his heart for what was next.

The plan Paul and the sailors came up with sounds crazy, but it worked. If you've ever been trained in open-water sailing, you might recognize how it would work. They looked for an island to run the ship aground. Then they waited out the storm. The only problem was they hit a hidden sandbar, and the ship started to break apart.

Imagine, just as their plan was coming together, it all fell apart. Ever been there? I know I have. But that didn't break their concentration or courage. Instead, they abandoned ship. They swam for the shore. They grabbed on to anything floating and beat against the current.

Sometimes when our best-laid plans start falling apart, we just need to swim against the current. We need to buckle down and give it all we've got. And other times we need to grab on to something and hold on for dear life. That thing we hold on to is usually someone else. We find someone who's been through what we've been through. We see the lifeline they throw out and grab it. The thing is, later on, after our shipwreck, we get to be the one who throws out the lifeline. It's incredible how God works!

The end of this chapter in Acts is the beginning of a new story. They all made it safely to shore and were rescued. But then for Paul, another challenge lay ahead. Rome. Caesar. And possible death. Would Paul be up for it? His struggle wasn't his end. His life was a series of struggles, almost constant and unrelenting. There were times when the wind was in his sails, and there were times when it was in his face. Our lives are the same way.

But he knew to rejoice in every struggle. Why? Because it produced endurance for the next one. You might so wish that God would just sort of beam you out of whatever struggle you're currently in. But he doesn't. Do you know why? It's because he loves you.

God loves you enough to let you continue through your struggles. They make you stronger, they increase your strength, and they define your hope. If we look at every struggle like it's the end, it just may be. We can stop dead in our tracks. But when we rejoice in the face of our struggles, they will lead us on to the next victory. It's all in how you view your situation and circumstances. It takes zeroing in on God in the midst of your struggle. Consistently training your ear to his Word will keep you afloat. And leaning on his rest will keep you moving.

Take a few minutes to think about some struggles you have been through.

Now build your faith by listing how God has used those challenges to teach you new principles and work something good from a bad situation. What struggles do you currently have? Look at how God has been faithful before. Imagine some ways that God may create opportunities from your current circumstance.

CHAPTER 5

failure is not the end

Let me tell you the story of one of the greatest military defeats of all time. This is a story of a decorated officer who made a series of bad mistakes, dumb moves, and terrible maneuvers that resulted in loss of life and ground. After you hear this story, you'll wonder why this person was ever put in charge of a military command to begin with. You'll also be at a loss to know why anyone would ever give him command again.

The twenty-two-year-old rookie officer was put in command of 159 troops though he had never faced battle before. One of this officer's first moves was a successful sneak attack. An advance scout had found a group of enemy troops moving through a nearby ravine. The officer decided to move swiftly. His men killed at least 10 of them and captured 21.

Confident about his first decision in command, he then decided to fortify his troops' position for defense against the enemy. Surely they would be planning a revenge attack. So within a meadow, he instructed his soldiers to build a round stockade. It couldn't hold all the troops, and many had to fend for themselves in a trench around the perimeter. The ground was soft from heavy rain that threatened to wash out the makeshift walls, and it was built so close to a wooded area that enemy sharpshooters were able to pick them off one at a time. But the recently promoted colonel still assumed the fort was well located for a defense.

The enemy attacked on July 3. By the next day, the battle was over. Completely humiliated and facing heavy casualties, the colonel finally surrendered.[5] It should have been the end of this young man's career. But it wasn't.

The year was 1754. The place was Great Meadows in present-day Pennsylvania. The colonel's name was George Washington. *The* George Washington, who would later rise to become a general. Who would take command of the Continental Army. Who would win battle after battle in the Revolutionary War. Who would become the first president of the United States.

He began his career with failure and defeat. But he knew something that we all need to know. He had the key that allowed him to keep moving, to be resilient in the face of struggle, to hold on to the hope of success with a death grip, and to never let his present circumstance define his future calling.

George Washington knew that failure isn't final.

it's not over

Your failure is never your end. If you keep going, you can gain strength from mistakes. Just like each struggle can build endurance, each failure can create momentum.

We've covered the circumstances we find ourselves in and the situations we often put ourselves in. We have to see both of those things clearly, through the lens of hope in God. When we do, we can understand our struggles.

So let's get serious here. Let's talk about what happens when we buckle under those struggles. When you fail, it feels awful. Sure, the struggle is over, but it's worse because you missed it, you messed up, you made mistakes, and now you're on the sideline. You're stuck.

Let's get honest about those failures. What is your greatest failure? Go ahead and name it. Don't hide it. Face it! For most of us, this is a difficult question to answer. We don't like admitting our mistakes. We hate reliving our worst moments. We just want to get over past pain and move on. For some of you, that failure may have cost you more than you want to admit. A mistake at work might have meant a lost job. A lapse in judgment could cost you your marriage. A terrible tragedy ends up leveling your house. It could happen. I understand.

I was invited to a pastor's gathering in Chicago in 2015. The other invited pastors led some of the largest churches in the US, the biggest averaged over twenty thousand people per Sunday. I felt way out of my league. The population of the town I grew up in was only 244.

The leader of the retreat asked me to begin one of the days with a devotion. I wanted to do something memorable because I was hoping to create meaningful connections with the other church leaders in the room. I decided to try to memorize a long passage of Scripture the night before. The next morning, when it was my turn, nerves kicked in, and I totally misquoted and jumbled up the Bible. This is not an acceptable practice by those in ministry. I got super flustered and started sweating. I'm not sure what I said during the devotion, but I'm certain it wasn't as meaningful as it could have been. I was embarrassed. I felt like the biggest failure.

No matter how big your failure feels, it's not final. And if it's not the end, then it can only mean one thing. Each failure is a new beginning. Something else is on the horizon. God will stir something new within you. Something you were made for. It's never over. It can only be a new something.

God stirred in me the responsibility of preparation. He also showed me there are second chances. As I type this, I am at the twentieth gathering of this group of pastors. I have been invited to ten of the events, more than anyone else. God was shaping something really special in me through my failure.

save point

Video games are pretty great. I know that some people can get a bit obsessed, spending too much time on them. But programmers actually create video games so you can play them for short bursts at a time. It's built into every video game. It's called a save point. A save point is a place in a game where you can stop and continue later at the same spot. You don't have to restart from the very beginning. You don't lose all the work you've done or the achievements you've earned. Instead, you pick up right where you left off.

That's what makes video games so fun, I think. Because of save points, you can be bold. You're never afraid of failure. If you mess up, oh well. You can go back to that save point and start again. You can face any danger in the game, go as fast as you want, make as many daring jumps as you need to. Why? Because if you fail, it's not the end.

I know that save points don't exist in real life. We can't go back and just relive the day, trying not to make the same mistakes again. It would be cool if we could though. But we are left with the reality we live in. And that reality gives us three options when we fail.

One: you can quit. Just give up. You hit the wall and decide it's not for you. Whether you quit that project, your job, that relationship, whatever. Quitting is always an option. But quitting is a guarantee that you'll never know the sweetness of success.

Two: you can start over. Just hit restart on that area of your life. Take on another job, start a new project, go on a date with someone else. That's pretty attractive. It's like starting over with a clean slate. The problem is that those who just want to hit restart usually don't learn from their mistakes. They avoid looking too deeply at their failures. They just want to move on.

Three: you can get stronger. You can push into your failures and learn from them. You can double down at your job, make a fresh go at that same project, or reinvest in that relationship. It's the hardest of the three choices, sure. But it's really the only way you can use each failure as momentum to reach your true potential.

Now let me ask you the tough spiritual question. Which of those three options do you think God wants you to do? It may be tempting to say the second since he promises us a clean slate from our past. But I'm not talking about your salvation from sin. I'm talking about your recovery from failure. What does God want you to do? The God who says he will redeem what you lost (Joel 2:25). The God who asks you to make the most of every opportunity (Colossians 4:5). The God who says he will renew your strength when you fail (Isaiah 40:31).

What do you think that God wants you to do?

I think he wants us to get up off the ground, dust ourselves off, and take another run at that wall. I think he wants us to be resilient, determined to make it work. I think he wants us to see failure not as an end but as a new beginning.

Save points don't exist in real life—not really. But I do believe that God can create them for us. He can provide an opportunity for us to take back what we have lost. To keep moving forward without having to live our entire lives over again. To start fresh each day with a renewed energy from his grace and mercy.

Do you believe me? Maybe not. That's why we need to look at an example in Scripture to get completely clear on it. A story of some person to whom God gave save points. I know just the person. His name is David, and he's one of the most incredibly righteous and incredibly tragic people in the whole Bible.

returners of the lost ark

David was a man in the Bible who had huge success! But he also had some huge failures. He was a shepherd boy, a mighty warrior, and a great king. We celebrate all his successes, beginning with how he killed Goliath with just a slingshot. But how about his failures?

You might have heard about that fling he had with Bathsheba. But did you know it was only part of a pattern of marital infidelity? Or how about the times his heart was divided between his own ambition and devotion to God? You may have never heard a sermon on the census he took that nearly destroyed his kingdom. We like to view our heroes in the best light possible. But it's when we are honest about their failures that we have confidence to see our own failures through God's sight.

In 2 Samuel 6 we read a story about failure before success. It's another mistake David made, and it was a pretty big one. He followed it up with an incredible success story that can't go unnoticed. That success, however, was only possible because of how he saw his own failure. Let's back up to give you some context about this story. While in the wilderness, God instructed Moses to build a tabernacle, or a tent, where God would meet with his people. They would sacrifice to him, and he would hear their prayers. The centerpiece of the tabernacle was the ark, a gold-covered chest that represented God's throne and presence among his people. This would be their most prized possession. You probably know about this from the 1981 movie *Raiders of the Lost Ark*. The hero, Indiana Jones, went to find this relic from the past that supposedly held tremendous power.

Once they came into the promised land, the Israelites fought fiercely against their enemies. On one occasion, the Philistines were defeating God's people. So the Israelites decided to bring God into the battle with them. How? By marching the ark from the tabernacle into the field of battle (1 Samuel 4).

You might remember from the movie that the ark was opened and this incredible power was released, killing Nazis in the Egyptian desert. Well, that's Hollywood and not reality. The tremendous power of the ark was not a weapon but God's visible presence among his people. During this battle, however, the

Israelites were not careful to consecrate themselves. Just because they had the ark didn't mean they had God's presence. They lost the battle, thirty thousand men died, and the Philistines captured the ark. It was gone. The presence of God was missing from the tabernacle; the glory had left Israel.

Fast-forward twenty years to when David was king and he decided to go and find the ark, returning it to the rightful place in the tabernacle. What started out as a great idea, a noble endeavor, a true calling from God, soon turned into tragedy and failure. Finding the ark wasn't hard, and carrying it back shouldn't have been either. But David was not careful about the presence of God. This is what he did: "They placed the Ark of God on a new cart and brought it from Abinadab's house, which was on a hill. Uzzah and Ahio, Abinadab's sons, were guiding the cart that carried the Ark of God" (2 Samuel 6:3–4).

Doesn't sound too bad, does it? That was probably a good plan. Except it wasn't God's plan. He had laid out very specific instructions for how the Israelites were to carry the ark—by priests using poles. Instead, David's men put it on an oxcart, and Uzzah and Ahio were not priests. It's very interesting that this is the exact same way the Philistines carried the ark away from battle. Instead of God's way, David chose the world's way. We can become so focused on success that we neglect to follow God's clear guidelines. We see worldly success and decide to use worldly schemes and strategies. What we need to do is to listen closely to God's Word and follow him.

David didn't listen. And it cost his people a life. "When they arrived at the threshing floor of Nacon, the oxen stumbled, and Uzzah reached out his hand and steadied the Ark of God. Then the LORD's anger was aroused against Uzzah, and God struck him dead because of this. So Uzzah died right there beside the Ark of God" (2 Samuel 6:6–7).

Huge mistake! Big failure! David's mismanagement, his selfishness, and his arrogance cost him big time. Would he be able to recover from this level of failure? Of course he did. David took some specific steps in order to go from failing to winning. Let's take a look at each one. Next time you find a failure in your life, here's how to refocus for success.

1. admit your mistakes

David had a hard time doing this. What was his first response? Anger. David was enraged! At himself? Nope. He was mad at God for killing Uzzah. He was so mad that he abandoned his plans and left the ark of God at the house of Obed-edom, an Israelite living in Gath. We often want to place the blame on someone else. We love to deflect our own mistakes. I think there is some fear involved. If we admit that we messed up, then maybe we're admitting that we are a mess up. But freedom comes when we take responsibility.

This happened in my life recently. A Sunday school teacher was going to be away and unable to teach her class. I knew she was going to be out of town, and she thought it was sufficient to tell me. I'm not usually involved in the logistics of Sunday school. When no one showed up to teach her class, one parent was very upset. Instead of taking responsibility and finding a solution to the problem, I pointed out that the Sunday school director should have solved the problem. I was trying to off-load the situation onto someone else when, in reality, it was my fault. The courage that it takes to admit your mistakes and accept responsibility releases soul toxins. In this situation, I quickly realized what I was doing and apologized to everyone involved.

Failure is never not an option. Following God can be risky. When you take on that challenge, you may find yourself making a mistake, taking a misstep, messing up royally even. The longer it takes you to admit your mistake, the longer you will stay out from under God's blessing.

Guess what happened to Obed-edom, the man with whom David left the ark. God blessed him and his household! In the three months that the ark stayed there, they saw increased favor from God. The favor that was meant for David and the rest of Israel God had redirected. Why? Because it took David three months to admit his mistake.

If you live any length of time, you will fail. Instead of being embarrassed, embrace it. If you have someone in your life trying to shame you for your failures, it probably means they're ashamed of their own failures. We all make mistakes. It's a fact of life. Those who grow are those who admit their mistakes. Those who never admit failure are cursed to repeat it over and over again.

2. quit replaying your past

Failures seem to have a long shelf life. It's hard to shake them off. When God killed Uzzah, it really got under David's skin. He decided to stop right there and name that specific piece of land. He called it *Perez-uzzah*, which literally means "to burst out against Uzzah" (2 Samuel 6:8). God burst out in anger with David, and Uzzah was the recipient.

I can just see David letting that failure run through his mind. Every time he traveled through Perez-uzzah, he remembered it. Whenever he met someone from there, a cold chill went down his spine. Anytime someone just mentioned the name Uzzah, he felt a fresh wash of failure. We all have a Perez-uzzah in our lives. One huge mistake that meant monumental failure. We can let it hamper us every time we walk near that place, or we can keep going right on by. It's up to us.

People may love to remind you of when you failed. They may stay quiet about your successes. Don't let that affect you. Your failures don't define you. So don't let memories of them lead you. Sometimes I think about my most sinful moments and disqualify myself from being used by God. The Enemy can use the memories of the past to remind us of our sinful nature. We forget that God spreads our sin "as far from us as the east is from the west" (Psalm 103:12) and that we are the righteousness of God in Christ.

Researchers have found that we are better at remembering the bad things we do than the good that happens to us.[6] In fact, good memories are the most easily forgotten, while bad ones stick to us like glue. We can't all stop our brains from working this way. But we can stop ourselves from dwelling on the past. David could have done just that, kept running it over and over again in his head. Maybe he would have cast more blame on God. Or maybe he could have piled more shame on himself. See, there's a difference between remembering our mistakes and dwelling on them. While David couldn't forget the mistakes he made, he chose to accept the forgiveness God offers and move forward, using the memory of his poor decisions as a reminder of his reliance on God rather than a roadblock. How do we know? Instead of leaving the ark in Obed-edom's house for another three months or longer, David decided to act. You can't act if you're too busy running the tapes.

To be a true leader of God's vision for his life, David had to relinquish the past. Don't dwell on your past failures. Focus on God's plan for your future instead.

3. improve your decisions

The best way to move on from your past is to look forward to your future. Find ways to make better choices. If you keep running the same mistakes over and over through your mind, switch it by thinking about how to make good choices just ahead.

You need to have a "plus one" mentality. Proverbs 24:16 says, "The godly may trip seven times, but they will get up again." That means you don't have to count your failures; you just have to count "plus one." *I failed at this task. Plus one more attempt.*

I made a mistake. Plus one more try. I messed up. Plus one more good choice.

David finally began learning from his mistakes. He gathered all his officials together and talked it over. Then he went to the priests and Levites and made sure he had the right plan in place. Finally, he called on all Israel to intercede and be ready to worship. Once he did that, he was ready for his plus one. He stopped dwelling on the past. He made a new plan with good choices. And then he moved forward.

Now get this. He lined up the Levites to precede the ark with trumpet blasts. Then he got the priests who were assigned to carry the ark into position. Once that was all set, he had the whole group move forward. Then, after only six steps, he stopped them. Only six steps, almost like he forgot something. But he didn't. He had it all planned out. "After the men who were carrying the Ark of the LORD had gone six steps, David sacrificed a bull and a fattened calf" (2 Samuel 6:13).

Isn't that awesome! Before they took one more step, David made sure to acknowledge God. He put God in the proper place, right in the center of their hearts. And then they moved forward in triumph. This was David's statement about defeat. He knew that his failure was due to self-centered and arrogant thinking. Now he needed to learn from that defeat and put God in the center. Only through the Lord's strength could David take one more step. Only because of his God could David give a plus one.

Your success is always on the other side of failure. Think about it! No one was ever truly successful until they failed—and failed a lot! Because until you fail, you don't know what you can't do. You only know what's easy to do, what's well within your grasp. But once you start moving to higher levels of achievement and things get more and more difficult, you won't know what you can't do until you fail. Then you get up again, you keep trying, and you keep improving. You get better! That means you can't really get better until you fail.

If you're learning a musical instrument and only practice the songs that you don't make mistakes playing, you'll never improve. If you're playing basketball and only take the shots you know you'll make, you'll never be a star. If you're starting a business and you only take the safe route, you'll never find true success.

Bart was an executive leader at Central Christian Church. Central is one of the largest churches in the US and is often looked to as a pacesetter for other congregations in their movement. Doug was an executive pastor at Canyon Ridge, another wildly successful church averaging an attendance of over six thousand on a typical Sunday. They shared a dream of a movement of churches using a similar set of leadership principles to advance the Great Commission. Together, they felt the Holy Spirit ask them to start a ministry to help one thousand churches per year, reaching a million new lives for Christ.

Bart and Doug left their comfortable and exciting church jobs to pioneer something new. They called it Intentional Churches. Today Intentional Churches is getting closer and closer to helping one thousand churches per year, utilizing a set of tools called ChurchOS. They are often featured at large church conferences and even landed a book deal with a major publisher. They went all in on it because they felt God was there with them. They knew that failure was possible. Their families supported them but also thought they were a little crazy. The early days certainly had struggles, but instead of giving up, they kept pursuing their God-sized dream.

When you are ready to fail and see your failure as an opportunity for new growth, then you're putting yourself in the right spot for God to bless you. He wants to use you but only when you admit that you can't do it alone. Failure is God's way of showing us how much we need to rely on his strength.

CHAPTER 6

it's bigger than you

Have you ever thought about changing your name? It's a big decision. But almost everyone goes through a phase where they wish they had a different name. At the very least, you may prefer a nickname over your real name.

A lot of athletes like to go by their nicknames. A lot of singers and musicians have stage names. Katy Perry's real name is Katherine Hudson, but she was afraid that if she called herself Katy Hudson, people would confuse her with the actress Kate Hudson.[7]

Many actors change their names for one reason or another. Most of the time it's so their name is just easier to say, spell, and remember. Do you know the actor Michael Keaton, star of movies like *Mr. Mom*, *Night Shift*, *Beetlejuice*, and *Batman*? That's not his real name. His real name is Michael Douglas. But when he was starting out as an actor and entered the actor's union, there was already a famous actor named Michael Douglas who had come before him.[8] Of course, that actor was called Michael Douglas only because his father, Kirk Douglas, had changed his name years before. Kirk Douglas's real name was Issur Herschelevitch Danielovitch.[9]

You know what? I may have changed my name, too, if it were that long.

In the Old Testament, names were pretty important. You got your name because of some characteristic that your parents saw in you, even from birth. And you carried that name with you for the rest of your life. If you had a name with a lot of baggage, then you'd probably be carrying that baggage your whole life.

There was one man in the Old Testament who was carrying a lot of baggage because of his name. He was born to rich parents, in prosperous surroundings, under the blessings of God. His name was Jacob, Isaac's son, Abraham's grandson. The name *Jacob* means "liar," "thief," "no-good." He had everything that he could ever hope to get from life. But his name stuck with him, and he ended up losing it all only to get it all back later in life.

from the day he was born

In science and sociology, there's a big debate about why we do the things that we do. Maybe you've heard about it or even studied it yourself. It's called "nature versus nurture." Are we born the way we are, which is the argument for nature? Or are we made the way we are, nurtured that way? The debate is usually about bad behavior. Are drug addicts a result of their environment? Or are they born with a chemical makeup that causes them to rely on drugs? Are some people destined for a life of crime because of their DNA? Or are all criminal minds formed by their experiences?

It's a hotly debated subject, and no one has a real answer. Maybe you've thought about your situation, the environment you grew up in, and you feel helpless. Or maybe it's the circumstances you've brought on yourself because of bad choices. Either way, you think that it's bigger than you. There's just no way out of the nature you have or the nurture you've gotten.

Well, in the case of Jacob, he had both happening to him. Just look what happened when he was born along with his twin brother, Esau. "Then the other twin was born with his hand grasping Esau's heel. So they named him Jacob" (Genesis 25:26).

And in this way, his parents stuck the kid with a bad reputation. From the day he was born, he was called Jacob the heel grabber, thief, liar, swindler. All those bad things wrapped into one name and then hung around this baby's neck. He started living up to that name too. One day Esau was out hunting, and Jacob was at home cooking. When his brother came in from the fields starving for something to eat, Jacob made a very one-sided deal with him. "Give me your birthright," he demanded. "Everything you will inherit from our father will be mine, for just one bowl of soup" (Genesis 25:27–34).

Was Jacob just born that way, a prisoner of his own genetics? Or was there more to it? As you keep reading in Genesis 27, you find that he was also nurtured to follow that path of jealousy and deceit. While Isaac, Jacob and Esau's father, was lying blind on his deathbed, we find out that Rebekah, the boys' mother, had been whispering in Jacob's ear the whole time. She helped him come up with a plan to steal not only the birthright but also the blessing of the firstborn, which belonged to Esau. She dressed her favorite son, Jacob, in his brother's clothes. Then, Jacob sneaked into Isaac's room with some food Rebekah prepared, and he pretended to be Esau to gain the best blessing.

A liar. A thief. A criminal. Was he just born that way, or was he made to be like his name? Either way, he felt it was bigger than he was. He felt lost and out of control. And his actions led to huge strife between him and his brother. So he fled from his family and home. That jealousy and deceit that he used to gain a birthright and a blessing seemed to result in him losing both.

Maybe sometimes you feel like you're out of control. You think that you were just born with a propensity to sin, and we're talking big sins. Not little white lies but schemes and scandals.

You started out with small things, like swiping a candy bar when no one was looking, and now you've graduated to worse. You cheat on your spouse. You abuse your children. You lie about coworkers to get ahead. And it's just been snowballing your whole life.

Instead of getting ahead, you realize this pattern of life is bigger than you ever imagined. You feel distant from friends and family. What you always wanted was taken from you just as it was within your grasp because you never dealt with the problems. You let them escalate, and now you've lost all control. And you can't take one more step. You're lost and all alone.

inside and outside

We are all products of forces we can't see. Some of them come from inside us, like the nature that we are born with. Others are from outside, the nurture aspect that shapes us as we live our lives. All of us are born into a broken world, but we are also born with broken souls. We have a sin nature within that leads us down the path of disobedience. And we all willingly indulge it when we give in to temptation. These two forces are at work on all of us, whether we know it or not, whether it's visible or invisible.

The internal and external struggles we face are like weights around our neck. They hold us back. Even when we think we're moving forward, they keep us stuck in neutral. They prohibit us from truly gaining freedom in life like we know we can have and want to enjoy.

Our internal struggles just add to the external pressures we feel. They complicate one another and lead to a life that's less than ideal. We end up just short of what God has for us, and we imagine these struggles are just so much bigger than we are. How can we possibly move forward?

My friend Bob knows all about being stuck because of the internal and external struggles in life. Born and raised in

McLeansboro, Illinois, he had been a member of a church I pastored for much longer than I have been alive. In 1970, he gave his heart to the Lord and felt a wave of change sweep over his life. He knew that from that day forward, nothing would be the same. He encountered the same God who offered grace and rest to Adam and Eve after they sinned. And now his own life would be transformed by that same grace.

Shortly after accepting Jesus into his life, Bob felt called to contribute to missionary work overseas. After exploring several opportunities, he found out about a project the General Baptist church was doing in Jamaica called Faith Home. It's an orphanage founded on Christian principles. For ten years, Bob prayed for the children there, supported several orphans, wrote letters, and sent money. Finally, he decided to go there himself. He boarded a plane and headed for Jamaica. But once he landed in Kingston, he realized something dark that he had hidden deep inside.

In the small town where he was born, raised, and still lives, there weren't many people of color. He never really thought about his own prejudices, but they were there just under the surface. Were they a product of his environment or just an extension of his own sin nature? He wasn't sure.

Back in 1967, he had been drafted into the army and, for the first time, spent time around people of color. He started harboring bad feelings toward them. He began judging them not on the basis of their character or the image of God they bear but by the color of their skin. When he got out of the service, he didn't think much of it. He just moved back home and hid those prejudices down deep.

Fast-forward to that first trip to Jamaica. He was in for a rude awakening. He should have been prepared for it, but he wasn't. After all, most of us understand the population of Jamaica is predominantly Black. Bob felt the prejudice bubbling up inside him, an internal struggle he was fighting tooth and nail. He made his way to his room that night and wasn't sure what the rest of the week would hold for him.

He woke up the next morning to the sound of children playing. They sounded like any other children, but Bob knew there was something different about them. They were Black. He struggled to even get out of bed, frozen by his own internal prejudices. He made his way out to the courtyard, and almost immediately, a young girl walked up to him. Her name was Michelle. She reached out and touched his arm, rubbing her Black hand along his white skin. She looked into his eyes and smiled. At that moment, Bob felt something: love.

"All at once I could see how wrong I had been in my life," Bob told me about that day. "God gave me a love that I never had before."

He realized right then that the prejudice he had been holding on to was sin. Racism had found an anchor-hold in his heart. He also knew he didn't want to give it room anymore. From that time on, Bob began to soften and open his heart to people of color. He named and denounced his sin of racism and repented of the internal issue he had long ignored. But that wasn't the end of his story.

Our internal struggles can often amplify our external ones. Bob had a special place in his heart for Faith Home in Jamaica. But soon after he visited, the government took over, and the General Baptists made the decision to move the orphanage to Honduras. Bob and his wife were selected to direct the moving and construction efforts. Struggling with the external issues of bureaucratic red tape, problems with development, construction work, and finances for the new home, he felt his old internal issues coming up again. Now living among Hispanic people, he started reliving those same prejudices.

But when we handle our internal issues, it seems those external ones are removed as well. Bob began to fall in love all over again with a new group of children and people. Today, Bob is a celebrity in Honduras. The children and workers at Faith Home Honduras love him so much. In fact, many of them have named their children after him!

Racism is a sin issue, not a skin issue. Bob had to get over that internal problem before he could handle any external problems that came his way. But once he tackled it, he was empowered to move forward with confidence and grace.

a ladder we can't climb

Jacob had internal and external issues he had to deal with before he could move forward with confidence and grace. Those issues drove him far away. After fleeing from his brother, Jacob lay down and slept. And he dreamed. He saw the skies open up and a long ladder coming down from heaven. Angels were on either side, and the very presence of God was all around him. Here is what God told him:

> I am the LORD, the God of your grandfather Abraham, and the God of your father, Isaac. The ground you are lying on belongs to you. I am giving it to you and your descendants. Your descendants will be as numerous as the dust of the earth! They will spread out in all directions—to the west and the east, to the north and the south. And all the families of the earth will be blessed through you and your descendants. What's more, I am with you, and I will protect you wherever you go. One day I will bring you back to this land. I will not leave you until I have finished giving you everything I have promised you. (Genesis 28:13–15)

Now just for a second, imagine how incredible this must have sounded. The land you're abandoning? It's really yours. The family you're leaving? You'll soon have them back. The home you've always wanted? You already have it, even if you're homeless.

How could Jacob ever accomplish that? I think the answer was in that dream. The ladder that reached all the way up to heaven, there's no way Jacob could climb it. His internal sins kept him grounded on the earth. His external cares kept him weighed down. That ladder was bigger than he was. He could never reach the top. But as big as his problems were, there was a God who was bigger.

Maybe you feel like the sin inside you is bigger than you can handle. You keep falling to temptation. You want to change, but you just can't. You think your sin problem is too big for you to manage. You're right. Or maybe you feel like the problems outside you are just too much. The pressures in life are bigger than you and keep taking over. You're filled with worry and hamstrung by stress. You lash out in anger when things don't go your way. Or you retreat inside yourself, isolating from those who want to help. Those problems just seem too much for you to tackle. You're right.

Your internal and external struggles are too big for you to take care of on your own. But you weren't meant to. God created you so he could care for you. He is standing at the top of that ladder with his hand reaching down, wanting to help you up.

In John 1:51 Jesus calls himself the "stairway between heaven and earth." He's talking about that dream Jacob had over a thousand years earlier. Finally, God had come down to earth to do what we could never do. By his death on the cross, Jesus has completely dealt with our internal struggles. And in the power of his resurrection, we can withstand any external struggle we face. It is through Jesus, the man who is bigger than we are, that we can finally start moving forward.

temporary home or eternal hope?

Jacob eventually started a family and became wealthy. But those things could never take the place of the promise he left behind.

He clung to that dream and knew he'd one day return. But that meant facing his brother, the one he had lied to and stolen from.

Jacob started back home with his new family and livestock in tow. What would the future hold? Would he finally be held accountable for the sins that were always hiding within? Would his brother, Esau, have his revenge? Jacob had to stop for the night and rest. And when he did, he found himself stuck again. "Jacob…traveled on to Succoth. There he built himself a house and made shelters for his livestock. That is why the place was named Succoth (which means 'shelters')" (Genesis 33:17). Names. Again, names have such rich meaning in these stories. But regarding the shelter Jacob built for himself, was it an answer to his problems or a way for him to avoid addressing them?

What do we build around ourselves to keep from dealing with our problems within? What are you leaning on that will keep you from moving into what God has for you in life? Maybe you've talked yourself out of taking care of your internal struggles. It's easier to call them "issues" or "baggage" rather than confess them as sin. Or maybe you've allowed your fears to completely freeze you up. The unknown can be terrifying, often bigger than the threat itself.

Jacob faced those fears. He put aside his internal struggles and went out to meet his brother. And what he found was that Esau had already forgiven him. Jacob's worries and doubts were all unfounded. God had been preparing something even better for him than he could've imagined, something bigger than himself.

After that meeting with Esau, here's what happened with Jacob: "God said to Jacob, 'Get ready and move to Bethel and settle there. Build an altar there to the God who appeared to you when you fled from your brother, Esau'" (Genesis 35:1). The name of his final home was Bethel. The word *Bethel* means "house of God." It was where Jacob met with God, both as he was fleeing from his internal problems and after facing his external struggle.

Those names are important. He first stopped at Succoth, which was just a temporary stop along the way. It was a tent, a quickly made covering, never meant to be a forever home. Then he settled in Bethel, the place where God dwells. And where he wants us to remain as well. From Succoth to Bethel. From a shelter to a house. From temporary home to eternal hope.

We can give up if we think that our internal and external struggles are the end of us, that they are bigger than we are, and that there's no hope for us. We can search for shelter, something to cover us for the night. Or we can look for the eternal hope that will keep us forever.

Shelters against our problems will only keep us for so long. When we are stuck thinking those things are bigger than we are, we need to find something even greater. That's what we need to keep our focus on. If we can look forward to an eternal hope, we can keep going, get unstuck, and never give up.

This is what Paul said about persevering: "That is why we never give up. Though our bodies are dying, our spirits are being renewed every day. For our present troubles are small and won't last very long. Yet they produce for us a glory that vastly outweighs them and will last forever! So we don't look at the troubles we can see now; rather, we fix our gaze on things that cannot be seen. For the things we see now will soon be gone, but the things we cannot see will last forever" (2 Corinthians 4:16–18).

We don't have a problem with our struggles; we have a problem with our sight. What are we looking for? What are we fixing our gaze on? What are we staring at? We can either keep our eyes set on our temporary struggles or look to the eternal hope we have in God.

When Jacob fixed his eyesight, something else was taken care of. That name he carried with him from birth, that problem that dogged him his whole life, was finally settled. Every time he met someone new, he had to tell them his name. Jacob. Heel grabber. Liar and thief. But now that he was settled in the house of God, he received a new name. "Now that Jacob had returned from Paddan-aram, God appeared to him again at Bethel. God blessed him, saying, 'Your name is Jacob, but you will not be called Jacob any longer. From now on your name will be Israel.' So God renamed him Israel" (Genesis 35:9–10).

Israel means "God struggles for me." It means that no matter how big our issues are, God is always bigger. And God has decided to take them on for us. Jacob was a man who struggled with his internal sin problem and his external circumstances. He lived a long, lonely life until, one day, he gave those struggles to God. All it took was shifting his focus from the temporary to the eternal. His final home was one of hope.

How do we keep going? How do we get unstuck? We need to shift our perspective from our temporary troubles to our eternal glory. We need to shift our focus to something bigger than ourselves. We need to shift our eyes from what will one day be gone to what will last forever. And we can do that when we hand our struggles over to God.

CHAPTER 7

the possibilities are endless

In 1990, Dr. Seuss released *Oh, the Places You'll Go!* At the time the world didn't know it would be his final book. Maybe he did though. Apparently, he gathered up many of the unpublished doodles and drawings from his workshop, put them in a sensible order, and then wrote an extended poem about the paths life sends us on. He might have been cleaning up all the leftover art he could find, or maybe he was tying a final bow on his decades-long publishing career.

What was so unique about it was the main character. You probably know his other stars, from the Cat in the Hat to the Grinch. Then there are the Fox in Socks, Pop from *Hop on Pop*, and Horton who hears a Who. The list goes on. There seemed to be no end to the characters that came from Dr. Seuss's imagination. For his final book, though, he gave us his most unique and colorful character. The main star of *Oh, the Places You'll Go!* is you. No, not a person named "You" but you. The person reading this right now was the inspiration and star attraction of Dr. Seuss's final published work.

How does that make you feel?

Oh, the Places You'll Go! quickly rose to the top of the best-seller charts. It hit a chord with so many people, and it wasn't written for kids but for adults. It became a staple graduation gift from its first release. Every spring, sales of the book surge as grandparents, aunts and uncles, and even teachers buy them up for graduating students.[10] They scribble their own notes of encouragement in the inside front cover, then hand them over to those young people who are ready to go out and conquer the world, wherever they go.

The book is full of such encouraging words! It promises the readers that they will soar above the rest and become the best. I can just imagine a high school graduate opening that book for the first time. Someone gave it to them—maybe an older brother who went on to college first. They're confused a bit. "Why did you get me a children's book?" Then they read it and get excited, get inspired, get motivated. *Yes! I'm going to make something great of myself.*

So they load up their car for the long drive to college. They pack up some books and especially this book, maybe perched right on top. When they get to their dorm room, they find a special place for that book. Right on the shelf, *Oh, the Places You'll Go!* greets them each morning, is always there each afternoon, stares at them before they go to bed.

Oh, the Places You'll Go! But not yet. No, you're still in the waiting room. You're still stuck learning and planning and hoping. You'll go far! But not yet. Wait. Right here. And before long, that book is no longer a motivator. It's a weight. An anchor around that young person's neck, holding them down instead of catapulting them. Classes are tough, relationships tougher. The job market looks bleak, and inflation is on the rise. And soon they find themselves spinning their wheels. *Yes, I'll go places. But when? How long do I wait?*

Good old Dr. Seuss anticipated this. He added a couple of lines to help us see that sometimes that journey is a long and twisty one. He said that, despite the encouragement to soar above the rest, sometimes you won't. Sometimes we don't go places. Sometimes we sit and wait. And sometimes…we get stuck.

where were you going when you stopped?

All of us have a place God wants to take us. Places, in fact. We will all face struggles, encounter failures, and get hit with internal and external problems. How we handle them will determine whether we keep going or stay stuck. So if you're stuck, I have a question for you. Where were you going when you stopped? What goal did you have in mind that you didn't quite reach? What dream did God put inside you that hasn't been realized yet? What path were you trying to run down when your wheels found a rut and you hit a ditch?

We start out on our journey with high hopes. We imagine life at school to be successful and maybe easy. We picture the perfect job right in front of us. We hope for a better family, a better career, a better paycheck. But often those hopes are dashed.

School can be more difficult than we expected and much more boring than we ever imagined. That job is hard to find, and once we do, it's not what we thought it would be like. And family life? Well, that can be complicated. Let's just leave it at that.

So it's no wonder that so many of us slam on the brakes and let the engine idle for a bit. We end up taking a short break from going after that dream job, from dating, from being involved in ministry. But that short break can turn into an extended stay. And before we know it, we've lost all traction and momentum.

Colonel Sanders was sixty-two when he started Kentucky Fried Chicken restaurants. Martha Stewart didn't start building her homemaking empire until she was in her forties. *Little House on the Prairie* wasn't published until its author, Laura Ingalls

Wilder, was sixty-five. Singer Susan Boyle was forty-eight when Simon Cowell discovered her on the reality TV show *Britain's Got Talent*. The Marvel Universe didn't make an introduction until its creator, Stan Lee, was in his forties.[11] It's never too late to start pursuing what God has put inside you.

If Dr. Seuss had lived in the time of Paul, I'm not sure he would have written his book. Because tucked away in one of Paul's letters is a short sentence that seems to articulate everything Dr. Seuss wanted to say. "Now all glory to God, who is able, through his mighty power at work within us, to accomplish infinitely more than we might ask or think" (Ephesians 3:20).

get AMPed up!

When you hit neutral in life, what you need is a boost. Something to amplify your dreams and get you moving again. I think that's exactly what Paul was saying in Ephesians 3:20. He was talking to his close friends in Ephesus and encouraging them to keep moving. Don't stop! There's so much more ahead.

If you find yourself running in neutral, you need an amp too—an AMP. Those three letters stand for three attributes of God that Paul encouraged us with. Let's take a look at each one.

1. God is able

"Now all glory to God, who is able…"

Do you remember when Elijah faced off against the prophets of Baal in 1 Kings 18? Elijah told them all to call on their god while he prayed to the one true God. And whichever god answered with fire would be the winner. By the time it was Elijah's turn to pray, the prophets of Baal had shouted all afternoon, and nothing happened. Then Elijah called for the people to pour water over the altar. Not a smart move if you want God to send fire. But Elijah knew what he was doing. Elijah simply bowed his head, asked God to reveal himself, and then stood back and watched. God sent down a huge firestorm that consumed the water, the sacrifice, and the whole altar! God put himself on display for those who doubted he was able.

One quick prayer. One loud response. One mighty God! If God is able, he will answer you when you pray. If you believe that, you can have the worst situation and still trust that he can do it. If you believe that God is able to create the whole earth, solar system, galaxy, universe...then you have to believe he can help you live your life intentionally right now.

2. God is mighty

"...through his mighty power..."

One time, Jesus and his disciples got in a boat and crossed to the other side of the lake late at night. Jesus, tired from ministry all day, took a nap on board the boat. Suddenly, a big storm came up, and the winds began tossing the small boat around. It nearly capsized! The disciples were frozen with fear. They woke Jesus up. "Don't you care that we're going to drown?" they accused him (Mark 4:38).

Then Jesus looked to the storm and said one word. "Silence!" (v. 39).

The entire sea went calm, the boat came to a rest, and the disciples were left wondering, "Who is this man?...Even the wind and waves obey him!" (v. 41).

That's the type of mighty power we're dealing with when we pray to God. Jesus knew how deep the waters of that sea were because he created them. Jesus knew the speed of the winds because he set them in motion. Jesus knew the integrity of the boat because he holds all things together. God is not just able; he is also mighty. There is nothing too big for him. The Creator and Sustainer of all is ready to answer your call for help.

3. God is personal

"…at work within us."

It's great to serve a God who is able. It's awesome to serve a Jesus who is mighty. It's another thing to know a God who wants to be personal. What if I told you that the power that sent fire from the sky and calmed a raging sea could live inside you? You might think I'm talking about some sort of magic spell. But I'm not. I'm talking about the loving Holy Spirit, who abides within us when we choose to follow Jesus Christ.

We were doing an event in our church where we wanted to use balloons filled with helium as an object lesson. The idea was that we can give to God all the struggles we have. We would write them down on paper, tie them to a balloon, and let them fly into the air until they disappeared. The activity represented God's ability to erase our sin. The problem was that there was a national helium shortage. I went to our local dollar store hoping to find one of those birthday party–sized helium tanks. The young man working there, Elijah, was a college student who was not involved in any church.

The helium was nowhere to be found. I asked Elijah if they carried it. He said, "No, and I checked with our manager. She said we haven't had a helium tank in ten years."

The Holy Spirit, who lives inside me, nudged me to exclaim, "You're going to get one tomorrow." Good thing I said it without thinking because I quickly realized how crazy of a statement it was. I was thinking, *Oh no, word vomit got the best of me again.*

I talked a little while longer with Elijah, getting to know where he was with God. I learned that he still wasn't 100 percent sure about the reality of God. The next day he sent me a text that said, "You need to get down to the store." I rushed over to see what he wanted to talk to me about.

That day, after he finished unloading the store's weekly shipment, the truck driver realized there was one package Elijah missed. He yelled, "Hey, you missed a box!" The truck driver threw it to him. When Elijah looked down, he realized he was holding a box that contained a helium tank.

After he finished sharing the story, I said, "I guess this is a sign that God is real. You need to start coming to church now."

He never missed a week after that. He signed up to go on a mission trip to Washington, DC, and spent a few days at Arlington National Cemetery praying for people and sharing the gospel. A few months later, he moved away to a nearby city to finish his degree. I visited him to make sure he was plugged into a local church there, and he was. To this day, I keep that helium box in my office with Elijah's name written on it as a reminder of our personal God. A God who uses helium tanks to reveal his nature to us.

The reason we can say "I'm going to make it through any situation" is because of the power of the Holy Spirit within us. The reason we can believe that God has incredible, crazy, amazing places for us to go is because he will be going with us as his Spirit lives within.

Your dream may be great, too great even for you, but there is one who is greater within you. The presence of God makes all the difference in the world. God knows that, so that's why even after Adam and Eve disobeyed, God provided a special grace to them. They forfeited their place in the garden of Eden but not their place within the grace of God. Even then, God prepared in advance a way for us all to get back to that place where we can have a personal friendship with God.

supersize me!

What happens when we tap into God's AMP? In Ephesians 3:20, Paul said that we can "accomplish infinitely more." That's such a cool phrase. It's a bit hard to translate directly from the Greek. Here's what other versions of the English Bible have tried:

- "Immeasurably more" (New International Version)
- "Far more abundantly" (English Standard Version)
- "Exceedingly abundantly above all" (New King James Version)
- "Above and beyond" (Christian Standard Bible)

What does it mean? It means that you can't measure it even if you try. It means that it's more than more. Words seem to fail us—grammar is useless. It's so much! It goes above and beyond anything you've ever dreamed possible.

So why don't we act like it? Why do we let our dreams fizzle out into nothing? Why don't we get some boldness, amp up our prayer life, and go for it all? The problem is not our God but our perspective. I'm afraid we're thinking too small. We're believing too little. We're not asking for enough. We need to go up a size in our prayers. When was the last time you heard that? "When you pray, you should try to break the bank of heaven. Keep asking for more and more and more!" But that is exactly what God is telling us in this verse through the pen of Paul.

The 1990s were a different time. The word *grunge* described a genre of music. A new form of reality TV emerged in 1992. Disco music of the seventies made a comeback. And people were obsessed with toys like Beanie Babies and Tickle Me Elmo. There were some things in the nineties that were bad, like dial-up internet. If you've never had to wait for the rest of the household to get off the phone so you could get online, you've never experienced life in the nineties. But there were also some very good things too. Fast food was great back then! And mostly because of one word: *supersize.*

I hope you're old enough to recall the golden days of the Golden Arches. But if not, let me explain it to you. Back then, you could go into a fast-food restaurant and order your meal by simply saying a number. That's it. You barely had to communicate. A number three was a Big Mac, fries, and a Coke. Sure, that's pretty much how it is today. But the difference was that after telling the cashier your number, they would ask you, "Do you want to Supersize that?"

Supersize meant that the regular was not enough. In fact, large was still too small. Supersize was an extra large. When your meal was ready, the tray would be overflowing, nearly spilling onto the counter. The fries didn't come in that little paper sleeve. You got a cardboard container that could stand on its own. And then they'd hand you a bucket full of soda. You got more french fries than you should ever eat in one sitting, enough Coke to last you for days.

Supersize was the peak of nineties fast food. Then one day, it all came apart when a documentary filmmaker decided he didn't like it. Morgan Spurlock wanted to run a little experiment, and since he knew how to make movies, he documented it. For one month, he ate nothing but McDonald's food. He spent day and night, night and day, breakfast, lunch, and dinner at his favorite childhood restaurant. And every time they asked, "Do you want to Supersize that?" he would answer, "Yes."

I'll bet you can tell where this is going even if you have never seen his movie *Super Size Me*. He gained weight. A lot of weight. And after just a couple of weeks, his doctor warned him that his health was deteriorating. Supersizing nearly killed him. The same year the movie released, McDonald's workers stopped asking customers to order larger sizes and started offering smaller portions and healthier options.

While it is sometimes wise to downsize our food portions, our prayer life shouldn't be downsized. There's nothing unhealthy about supersizing our prayers. In fact, I think we need to supersize our prayers. We need to stop letting ourselves think our way out of prayer. I worry that many of our prayers go like this: *God, if it's your will and you would be glorified and you wouldn't be too put out…* God has already explained it to you. He wants you to pray big, bold, audacious prayers. He is a God who is able, mighty, and personally involved in your life. If the possibilities are truly endless, then we need to start praying like they are.

During my first ministry experience as the summer youth intern at the established, rural church with virtually no youth ministry, I could have taken one look at the single lightbulb hanging from the ceiling and doubted such an old, small church would ever have an active youth group. But the pastor had tasked me with getting something started for teenagers in that community. There were no real expectations for me, but I had some high expectations of myself. It was my first venture with any formalized ministry position, and I felt like if God is who he says he is, then I will believe he will do what only he can do. So I prayed for God to send us 50 students to minister to by the end of the summer. This was ten times the number that attended student functions.

Over the next two months, God breathed on that ministry, answering our audacious prayers. First 10 students, then 15, then 20. We began to see teenagers coming to know the Lord every single day—some coming into the church in the middle of the day after being drawn in by his power. As I saw God respond to my prayers, I asked and believed for more. Some of our worship gatherings grew to over 150 students in attendance—bigger than the Sunday morning attendance—with no more seating available in the pews, on the floor, or even in the balcony. Other youth groups from surrounding communities and even three other states brough vanloads of kids to our gatherings. We had a baptism service sixteen weeks in a row!

A few years later, I was asked to join the staff as a youth pastor at a fast-growing church. The church was just a few years old and had never had a formal youth ministry. The context was different, but many aspects felt similar to the experience I had as the intern. This time I prayed and believed for many more than 50 students. Our first gathering we saw 286 students show up, and every Wednesday after that was a supernatural outpouring of God's grace and incredible growth. God's faithfulness stirred my heart to walk in boldness. I believed God for the unimaginable and saw him do the impossible.

How do these big, bold, supersized prayers work? The last line of that passage in Ephesians 3 tells us God works "to accomplish infinitely more than we might ask or think." Prayer is the intersection between our imagination and inspiration. Paul said God's power within us goes beyond our asking and straight past our thinking. If you can imagine it, God already has it planned out. In fact, what you imagine may be too small. We need to allow God's ability, might, and personal involvement in our lives to transform our asking and thinking. We need our imagination to intersect his inspiration.

God is interested in running right past our own imaginations because it proves his inspiration in our lives. When we dream dreams that are just big enough for us, we can easily get the glory. But when we dream dreams that are bigger than we are, only God can get the glory.

Here's how Mark Batterson puts it in his great book *The Circle Maker*: "Prayer and imagination are directly proportional: the more you pray the bigger your imagination becomes because the Holy Spirit supersizes it with God-sized dreams...Nothing honors God more than a big dream that is way beyond our ability to accomplish. Why? Because there is no way we can take credit for it...If you keep praying, you'll keep dreaming, and conversely, if you keep dreaming, you'll keep praying."[12]

Dreams will help us reframe our situation into possibilities. We read the book *Oh, the Places You'll Go!*, and then we put it down and think, *Sure—someday*. But when we enter into prayer with a God who truly wants to answer them, our focus shifts. It moves from our situation and to our possibilities. It moves from our circumstances and to God's plan. It moves from our struggles and to our victory. It moves from our failures and to our opportunities.

Prayer moves mountains, but before it does, it moves our hearts. We start to shed the old, self-centered dreams and pick up new, God-focused ones. Guess which ones are bigger, by the way. You will never dream smaller than when you are the center of those efforts. But when you put God in the middle, the possibilities are endless.

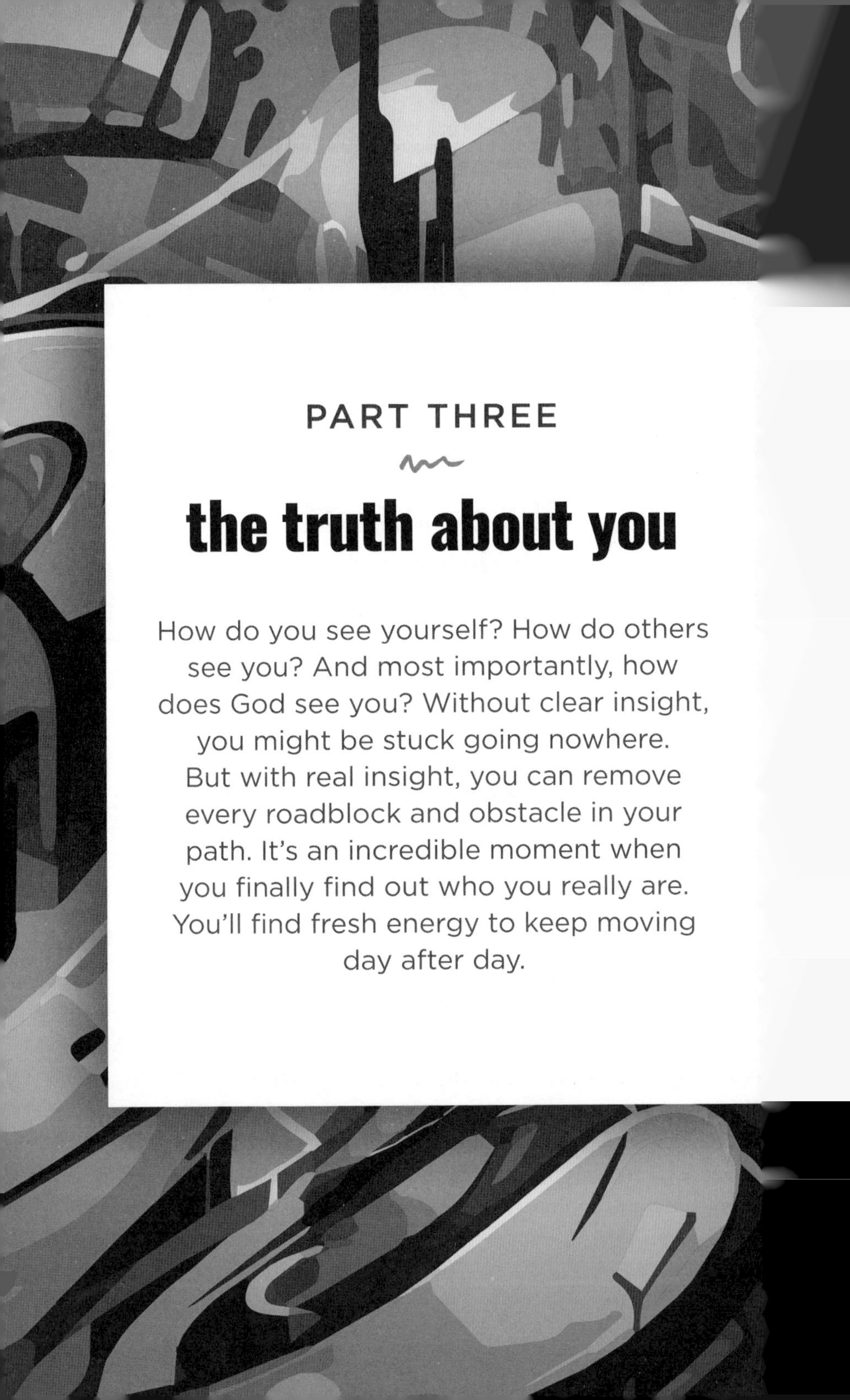

PART THREE

the truth about you

How do you see yourself? How do others see you? And most importantly, how does God see you? Without clear insight, you might be stuck going nowhere. But with real insight, you can remove every roadblock and obstacle in your path. It's an incredible moment when you finally find out who you really are. You'll find fresh energy to keep moving day after day.

CHAPTER 8

the dream God hides inside

When I took the position as senior pastor, I had no idea what I was in for. I loved the people and knew they were a great group of Christ followers who would love me back. I was excited to be a part of the community and help out however I could. So it wasn't my expectation of the people that was wrong. Not at all. It was my expectation of what I'd have to do each week that was way off. As a pastor, I am a preacher, a counselor, a worship leader, a friend. I have to know how to balance books and run a budget. I need to be able to motivate people and show appreciation. I may also have to mow the lawn some weeks or fix a leaky pipe, paint a wall, and even clean toilets.

There is not one thing wrong with any of that, and I welcome all of it! One thing that I realized very quickly that I needed to do was to cast a vision for the church. If you're in church ministry or you're close to someone who works at a church, then you know how crucial this is. Your vision must match the congregation's expectations and the community's felt needs. When you have the right combination, your church can make an impact in your area.

But vision is not just for pastors and churches. Vision is for you! Knowing who you are, what makes you tick, what you're good at, what you love to do—all those things build to your personal vision. When you find out why God put you where you are, gave you the gifts and passions you have, and allowed you to live the experiences you've been through, you can begin to be an influence on those around you.

Some call it a dream. Others stick with the vision terminology. I like either one because it's really all about seeing. How do you see yourself? If you don't have clear vision, you're stuck. You won't make a move. You're scared, frozen in your tracks.

You can never start moving in life without a clear vision for where you're going. But when you finally have your eyes open to who you really are, you can't wait to get moving. In the last section, we talked a lot about how seeing our circumstances for what they really are can help us keep moving, motivated, and resilient. Now we'll start to understand how we see ourselves.

the original vision caster

Vision leads to action. People with vision are people who move. And churches with vision are the ones that grow and lead others to spiritual growth. That's what churches should hope to be. Knowing that people within their reach zone wake up every day without the hope of Jesus, the question should be, How can we meet their needs?

That whole idea of casting a vision for your ministry didn't start in the late 1990s with Rick Warren. It goes back further than the 1950s, when many churches shifted to a more corporate way of doing things.[13] You have to go back further in time. Past the Second Great Awakening or even the First Great Awakening. Keep going right back through the Reformation. You haven't even scratched the surface yet. Here, I'll help you out. The idea of having a vision for your ministry goes all the way back to Jesus himself.

By the time you get to the fourth chapter of Luke, Jesus had just begun his preaching ministry. He hadn't upset the Pharisees yet. He had picked up a positive reputation for healing people—demons were cast out, those who were lame walked again, and even those who were blind could see. People loved Jesus, and they all wanted to see him. In fact, the gospel tells us that "he taught regularly in their synagogues and was praised by everyone" (Luke 4:15).

And that's where he was one Sabbath. He was sitting in a local synagogue in his hometown of Nazareth. The leader in charge of the service asked Jesus if he would read that day's Scripture text. So Jesus stood up, they unrolled the scroll of Isaiah, and he got right to it.

> The Spirit of the LORD is upon me,
> for he has anointed me to bring Good News to the poor.
> He has sent me to proclaim that captives will be released,
> that the blind will see,
> that the oppressed will be set free,
> and that the time of the LORD's favor has come.
> (Luke 4:18–19)

Now here's the cool part. Right after reading that part of the scroll, Jesus rolled it back up, handed it to the attendant, and then took a seat. He must have paused for dramatic effect because Luke tells us that all eyes were on him, waiting for what he'd have to say. "The Scripture you've just heard has been fulfilled this very day!" (Luke 4:21). In other words, "What I just read, you can stop waiting for. I'm here. I'm ready. Let's go!"

Jesus articulated his vision for ministry as clearly as possible. He knew that the Holy Spirit was on him. He had experienced that at his baptism. And he knew that his Father had given him a job to do, bringing good news to the world. He came to the poor, the captives, the blind, the oppressed. He came to tell them that God has unlimited grace for them, something Isaiah called "the time of the LORD's favor" (61:2). He knew what he was going to do, whom he was going to help, and how he would do it. And he knew all that because he knew what God had hidden inside him.

get the gloom out

I really like how James talked about this whole idea of seeing yourself. He compared getting a clear vision of what God has hidden inside you to looking into a mirror (James 1:23–25). That makes a lot of sense. A mirror will show you if you're ready to face the world. Maybe it reveals if you've got some problem, like a big zit or out-of-place hair. But mirrors can also be hard to face. If you don't like what you see, you might get stuck trying to fix it.

The big problem I have with mirrors is keeping them clean. Back in James' day, mirrors were really sketchy. They were basically big pieces of polished metal. Some were pretty good but not all. Not like the ones we have today. Of course, stepping out of a hot shower isn't good for looking in a mirror. It gets fogged up. You try to wipe it off, but that just streaks it. If you're like me, your mirror is probably covered with a few months' worth of toothpaste and flossing shrapnel. I guess I should leave the Windex in the bathroom. That's the one place I need it most.

Having a foggy or dirty mirror is not good for keeping up your appearance. But having a messed-up spiritual mirror is even worse. It keeps you from seeing your vision clearly. The prophet Isaiah, the same one whom Jesus quoted in Nazareth, put it this way: "In that day the deaf will hear words read from a book, and the blind will see through the gloom and darkness" (29:18). The day he was talking about is when God brings salvation to his people. It could mean in the past, when the nation of Israel finally returned from captivity. It could mean that day Jesus spoke of, when he came to earth the first time. It may even refer to a future time, when Jesus finally comes back for all of us. It could even be referring to all three.

In fact, I'd add a fourth. I think that anytime someone comes to believe in Jesus, this verse is for them. They were spiritually deaf, but God opened their ears to really hear his words. They were spiritually blind, but God healed them so they could truly see. Good hearing and good vision, that's what it takes to keep moving forward—growing in faith and fulfilling your dreams. God brings us out of gloom and darkness. That's what his prophet told us. When we choose to follow his leading, he removes all the gunk from the mirror, he wipes it clean, and he shows us a clear vision of what he's hidden inside us all along.

gloomy gideon

The book of Judges is about, well, judges. But not the judges that you and I think of when we think of judges. The judges in the book of Judges didn't wear black robes. Some of them did resolve conflicts, sure. But most of them were called by God to lead his people, the Israelites, in battle against their enemies.

Those judges had to be tough, like Samson. He was probably the strongest judge of them all. He had superhuman strength. He had bulging muscles, a military mind, and a ferocious grit. He would rip Philistines apart with his bare hands. But not all the judges could be superhero types. One guy, in fact, was pretty much the opposite. His name was Gideon. And although God called him a mighty man, he was more of a mouse.

Gideon was kind of a gloomy person. He definitely needed God to bring him out of gloom and darkness to really see who he was. And Israel needed someone with clear vision to help them against their latest enemies, the Midianites.

So here's what was going on. The Israelites were minding their own business, planting their crops, but whenever they did that, the Midianites would come in on horses with swords and shields and scare them away, stealing their crops and ruining their fields. The Midianites left the Israelites with nothing to eat. They robbed them of their sheep and cattle and goats too. They were as thick as locusts, the Bible tells us. And Israel was on the brink of starvation (Judges 6:2–6).

Did you know the world is starving? I know that there are places on earth undergoing incredible food shortages, terrible droughts, and poverty that prevent even little children from having enough to eat. But I'm talking about another type of famine.

There is a famine in the world of the Word of God. There is a shortage of love, an absence of joy, and a deficit of peace. The Enemy has stripped people of their hope and left them helpless. And unless they hear the truth from someone who knows—like you and me—they have little chance of spiritual survival. God is calling us today, just like he called Gideon thousands of years ago.

Will we see his vision clearly? Can we interpret his dream that was hidden inside? Or will we make excuses just like Gideon did? That's right. I told you Gideon was gloomy. When the angel of the Lord showed up to give Gideon his big plan, he found Gideon hiding out. He wasn't just hiding out; he was threshing his grain in a winepress. What does that mean? Well, let me tell you. And I only know because I looked it up. In those days, they threshed wheat out in the open. To thresh wheat—and I'll bet some of you already know this—is to separate the husk from the kernel inside. The kernel is what you eat. The husk? That's just the hard outer shell. So they would beat the wheat, separating the kernel from the shell, and then toss it up in the air. The kernel would fall to the ground, and the shell would float off in the wind.

But Gideon? He was doing this in a winepress—a kind of shallow well dug in the ground where you would stomp grapes to get the juice. I don't know how this was going. It probably wasn't working too well. I'm sure his bread was pretty lumpy. But if he did this out in the open, the Midianites would see him and come steal his grain.

The angel of the Lord saw him hiding and said, "Mighty hero, the LORD is with you!" (Judges 6:12). And Gideon's response is great. Your version of the Bible may say something like "Sir" or "My lord." What I imagine him really saying is "Hey! What's going on? Who's there?" He was scared to death. He was afraid a Midianite had seen him and had come to steal his grain. He was the exact opposite of how you would picture a mighty hero. But the angel of the Lord was persistent. He told Gideon the plan, that Gideon was going to lead the charge to rid the Israelites of the Midianites. He told Gideon, "Go with the strength you have!" (v. 14).

The strength I have, thought Gideon. *You've got it all wrong, angel.* "How can I rescue Israel? My clan is the weakest in the whole tribe of Manasseh, and I am the least in my entire family!" (v. 15).

Gideon was gloomy. He couldn't see the truth. He couldn't find what God had put in him. And it kept him from moving forward. Instead of finding God's dream inside, he was hiding. Instead of standing on that promise, he was tearing himself down. And it was all because he just couldn't see clearly.

What can't you see about yourself? What's blocking your view? If you keep feeling stuck, I think some things in Gideon's story may be the same for you. If you have trouble recovering from hurts, moving past your past, or getting ahead when you fall behind, Gideon's attitude may just be your own. Take a look at some of these attitudes that Gideon had. Do you have one of them?

1. i'm too scared

This is so common. And trust me. We all get scared from time to time. I already mentioned how Mark Batterson feels we should pray big prayers. But those big prayers can scare us. Maybe God has given you some dream, and now you're scared. What will happen if you fail? What will change if you succeed? It's so big. Can it really happen?

Instead of letting fear keep you stuck in one place, let it drive you to the rest God has prepared for you. He has put the strength within you. When you get scared, go to him to find where he has hidden that strength.

2. i'm not good enough

I have a secret for you. We all feel this way sometimes. The most successful, the brightest, the best. Everyone who has ever done something great has had a moment when they didn't feel good enough.

I'm not saying I'm one of the best. Far from it! But I know what it's like to have a desire to do something great and get excited about seeing it happen. Then comes the crashing blow. That little voice inside whispers to you, reminds you of your past mistakes, and tears down that dream God is building. When you hear that voice, shut it up! Don't let it drown out God's Word in your life. Find yourself in the Bible. Read his promises to you. And block out those negative voices that say, "Someone else should do it."

The truth is that someone else will do it if you opt out. But God's dream is for you! He wants you to do whatever it is he put in your heart. But he will move on to someone else if you refuse to move with it. We all have an individual responsibility to make as much of our life as possible. And we only have one shot at it. Why not take that shot? Why not risk when the reward is so great? Why not go all in on the dream God put in you? When you feel like staying put, find a way to get moving. It may be one small step, like volunteering at your church. But that one step will lead to the next.

out of the darkness and into the light

Let's get back to Gideon—little Gideon who was hiding from the Midianites and tearing himself down. God gave him a plan—a dream, really—to take on the whole Midianite army. By the way, we know there were at least 135,000 troops in the enemy's camp (Judges 8:10). How many men did Gideon have? It looks like he was able to get 32,000 or so warriors for Israel. Those aren't great odds. Israel was outnumbered by over 100,000 men.

But wait. There's more. God then told Gideon to send anyone home who was scared. So 22,000 said, "See you later, Gideon," leaving him with only 10,000.

But wait. There's more. Then God had Gideon take his men to a stream to drink water. He told Gideon to separate the men who got on their knees to drink from those who lapped the water up from their hands, like a dog, their head on a swivel watching their backs. God knew what type of warrior he was looking for. One who kept his eyes fixed on the job. The problem was that only 300 men drank the water from their hands. That's not a typo. That's not an error. Gideon was left with an army of 300 men to take on the battalion nearly 500 times that size. Not good odds at all.

It's no surprise God gave Gideon instructions for what to do if he was afraid. Of course, he was scared! God told Gideon, "If you are afraid to attack, go down to the camp with your servant Purah. Listen to what the Midianites are saying, and you will be greatly encouraged" (Judges 7:10–11). Gideon, under the cover of darkness so no one could see, sneaked into the camp and right up to one of the tents. He and his servant Purah heard two Midianites talking. And here's what they were saying:

> The man said, "I had this dream, and in my dream a loaf of barley bread came tumbling down into the Midianite camp. It hit a tent, turned it over, and knocked it flat!"
>
> His companion answered, "Your dream can mean only one thing—God has given Gideon son of Joash, the Israelite, victory over Midian and all its allies!" (Judges 7:13–14)

I'm sorry, but that dream doesn't make much sense to me. Does it to you? Well, at least in our ears it doesn't. But I did some reading and found out some things that may help us here. First of all, the loaf of barley bread is not really a loaf like you and I think of it. It's not a package of Wonder Bread or a French baguette. It's not even a roll, which would make sense. The word for "loaf" might better be thought of as a cake, one that's rolled up and flattened out and then cooked on a flat griddle. Think of it like a waffle.[14]

So the Midianite saw an Eggo waffle come rolling into the camp. But not ordinary frozen Eggo. This was a barley waffle. And back then, no one liked barley bread. Think of it like one of those multigrain Eggos. I bet they sell more blueberry waffles than multigrain ones. I'm sorry, but no one really likes the taste of multigrain anything, especially waffles. So this multigrain Eggo—just go with me here—rolled into the camp and knocked over the tent. Why? Was it not tied down? What kind of tent can get knocked over by a frozen waffle? But the man's friend knew exactly what was going on in this dream. "A multigrain Eggo? That can only mean one thing. Gideon is on his way!"

Now we need to get some help here. How did they know about Gideon? And why were they making that connection? I have an idea. You see, people then thought of barley as food for peasants. And the Midianites considered all the Israelites to be beneath them. It looks like they came up with this nickname for Gideon—and not a good nickname either. Maybe they called him Ole Barley Loaf.

"Hey, did you hear that some little Eggo waffle is getting an army together?"

"Yeah, and not the good kind. This is some multigrain level of wimp!"

You know what? I'll bet Gideon even knew about that nickname.

"Gideon the waffle. He waffles back and forth because he can't make up his mind."

"Gideon the barley. He can...*barley* get an army together."

"Gideon the frozen. Look at him! He's hiding out in the winepresses!"

But the joke was on the Midianites. With only 300 men, armed with torches and jars, Gideon launched a sneak attack and routed his enemy. He ended up taking down the entire army, all 135,000 of them! And God got all the glory.

it takes a dream

Gideon was scared. He had every right to be scared. God knew that. Instead of telling him to suck it up, to grow some guts, to get brave, the Lord had him go listen in on a dream. Sometimes it takes hearing a dream to get moving. Sometimes when we're stuck, we just need to hear what others think about us, what they really see in us, or how God has revealed the same dream in another way. Sometimes it takes a dream. What's your dream? What are others saying about it? How can God use that dream to get you moving?

Gideon was hiding. He was stuffing all his grain down the chute of his winepress. But instead, God wanted him to see the dream he had hidden in Gideon's heart. God will reach for those places deep inside us to call us to do great things. Are you looking?

Gideon tore himself down. He called himself the runt of the litter. He was the youngest of his family, his family was the weakest of his tribe, and his tribe was the smallest of all Israel. But God didn't care. God saw the strength he put in Gideon, and he wanted Gideon to see it too. Gideon wasn't some frozen waffle; he was a decisive general ready to make a move. Did Gideon believe it? It took him a few tries. He asked God for a sign. And then another sign. Okay, one more sign. He followed God's orders though. To the letter. And it led him to a great victory. When we listen to God's orders—following the dream he placed deep within us—we can accomplish great things. Because we're doing it in God's power.

God knew that Gideon had some blind spots he needed to clear. We all do! But before we move on to identifying and dealing with them, let's first be encouraged that God wants us to see clearly. Psalm 146:8 talks about how much God cares for you. "The LORD opens the eyes of the blind. The LORD lifts up those who are weighed down." Are you weighed down? Do you find yourself tearing yourself down? Do you feel like the world has let you down? It's time to lift your head up, to open your eyes, and to really see.

CHAPTER 9

identify your blind spots

Have you ever had a problem with your eyes? I'm not talking about watery eyes or dry eyes. I'm not even talking about needing glasses. There is a condition called blepharitis that causes your eyelids and eyelashes to become irritated and swell. It can even produce stuff that looks just like dandruff but on your eyelashes. Maybe that's what Paul had when his eyes were scaled over after getting knocked to the ground on the way to Damascus in Acts 9.

Or what about chalazion? No, not calzone, the delicious cross between a burrito and a pizza. I'm talking about an oily lump that forms under your eyelid. It's not very fun, and it is pretty painful. Then there's myokymia, an uncontrollable twitching of the eyelid. It's a tic probably brought on by stress. I'll bet you've seen this before. I hope you've never experienced it.

Finally, I read about a condition with a name to it, Charles Bonnet syndrome. This is pretty common among people who had eyesight but then lost it. What happens is they hallucinate. They see something that's not really there. They think they can see, but they can't. Instead, their mind plays an image that they once saw. Almost like a rerun of the past.

Seeing things that aren't real—or not being able to see when you think you can—can affect spiritual insight as well. We need to have a clear picture of who we are if we want to keep moving forward in life. But sometimes there are things in the way of our view. We need to identify these blind spots.

can you see?

One day Jesus met a blind man in a village called Bethsaida. He wanted to heal the man of his blindness. But I think Jesus was also looking to teach us a lesson about our own blind spots. The lesson begins when the healing ends.

Jesus took the man outside the village. We're not sure why, exactly. Maybe he didn't want anyone to see what was going to happen next. Once he had the guy outside the village, Jesus spit on the guy's eyes. He laid his hands over them and then asked, "Can you see anything now?" (Mark 8:23).

Now if I were the blind guy, I think I would have said, "You mean did I see who just spit in my eyes? Are you asking if I can see that person?" But this man wanted to see. His friends had heard Jesus was in the area and was coming to town. So they had led the blind man right to the miracle worker. They believed! And he did too. So he opened his eyes. A million times before that day, nothing. He had seen nothing. He had perhaps lived his entire life in darkness. But that day it was all different. He opened his eyes, and he could see. At least he could see something. "'Yes,' he said, 'I see people, but I can't see them very clearly. They look like trees walking around'" (v. 24).

Maybe this man had Charles Bonnet syndrome. Maybe he was just seeing things, images of something in the past. What he had for sure were blind spots. This is exactly what so many of us experience in life. In the last chapter, we talked about how God has put a dream inside you. Can you see it? Sometimes it takes hearing someone else talking about it. It may mean letting someone else show you. Why? Because we may not be blind anymore, but we still have blind spots.

We need to take a good long look at ourselves. Can you make out the details? Or are there places that just don't quite come into focus? We were once blind, but now we can see—kind of. We can see well enough, right? We can see, but all those people look a lot like trees, not real people. We can see ourselves, but it's all covered up. It's smudged. It's not clear. We have blind spots in our lives. We need to identify them.

where are the blind spots?

We all have them. In your car it's that place just behind you and to the side that you can't quite see. You check your rearview and your side mirrors. But there's this one space that is just out of view of your eyes. In traffic, you had better check your blind spots. If you try to make a lane change without looking, you might crash. Or at the very least, you may get a not-so-friendly honk from the other driver. What they're really saying is "Hey, buddy! Watch where you're going!"

When we don't check our blind spots, we're driving on an assumption that we know everything or, at least, enough to make a decision and make a change. We believe that there are no other vehicles there. We believe that the way is clear. But we're not sure. We're not sure until we check.

Blind spots in your life are the same. They are areas of your life that you don't have complete knowledge of. You might think you know, but you don't. You may have a blind spot concerning your talent, where you think you're much better at something than you really are. You may have a blind spot of knowledge. You believe you have all the relevant information, but you're missing that one key piece. You might even have a spiritual blind spot, living under the assumption that your behavior is okay with God when it really isn't.

What can blind spots do? They have the potential to wreck your life. You make a move without checking your budget or making sure that job offer was all nailed down only to learn that you should have checked your blind spot. Now you're stuck without a job with a lease on a place you can't pay for. Or maybe you're in a relationship that has a blind spot. You thought he was the one, but it turns out he had his eyes set on someone else. You're blind to it until you're faced with the truth of a cheating boyfriend and a broken relationship.

But where do these blind spots come from? In a car, it's obvious. The manufacturer knows that the design of a vehicle will inherently include some blind spots, some areas outside the car that you can't quite see even with all your mirrors adjusted just right. We can have our own mirrors adjusted—we are spiritually in tune, we are tracking with God's Word, we are listening to him in prayer—but we still can't quite see that one area in our life. Why does this happen?

One way we form blind spots is by the way we see our past. We all suffer from selective memory. Have you ever noticed how much easier it is to remember the bad things and not the good? Our minds are made to warn us of danger. So they store the negative memories a little heavier, hoping we can avoid those things later in life. A blind spot is created in our memory. That's why so many psalms talk about remembering God and his good work in our lives. Because it's so easy to remember the bad that happens to us, we tend to forget the good that God gives us. A blind spot forms, and we think that God was never there through the bad times, that he never cared, and that we were always in trouble.

Another blind spot is how we learn new information. Confirmation bias is what researchers call it. We seek out information that confirms what we think about ourselves, what we believe about the world, or what we hope about God. So if you think you're not creative, you'll only listen to criticism. If you believe the world is full of evil, you'll focus on every fearful headline you can find. If you feel that God is unhappy with you, you might only pay attention to the parts of the Bible that talk about judgment, about the curse.

One more way that blind spots form in our lives is how we see other people. We like to put people into easily identifiable groups. This person kind of acts like someone who hurt us in the past, so stay away! A blind spot is formed around that person's individuality though. Again, it's our minds working to protect us.

One of the most abhorrent blind spots we can ever form is stereotyping. When we view others as just members of a particular group, we tend to make rash judgments about them. That includes ageism, sexism, and even racism. It's a damaging blind spot, a mark on our very hearts, because it denies that each person is made in the image of God. It denies God's good work in their lives. And it creates a negative sense of our self as well.

These blind spots all work together to shape your self-image. You look at all the bad things that happened in your life and ignore God's blessing. You fill yourself with news reports that just verify your fears. You believe the worst in others. And now you're left wondering why you feel so bad all the time.

Your blind spots are killing the dream God put in you. Blindness to God's past blessings keeps you from hoping for his best tomorrow. Blindness to good news in the world keeps you bitter. Blindness to true goodness in others keeps you locked in hatred and fear. There has got to be a better way.

don't believe your own lies

One of the ways your blind spots grow and get the better of you is through lies. It's bad enough to believe the lies of the Enemy, just like Adam and Eve did. It's worse to believe your own lies. We should know better. Sadly, we don't.

We all know about white lies. Those are the small, innocent, harmless lies we tell others. We know they're not true, but we say them anyway. Sometimes we don't even expect others to believe them. Your mom asks if you like her cooking. Your wife asks if that dress makes her look fat. Your friend asks if you think he's a good musician. We're all guilty of saying just what we think the other person wants to hear. It won't be that wrong. It's just a little white lie.

But there is another type of lie. A lie so desperate and deceiving that it goes through the entire spectrum of colors to the far end. Not a black lie, no. A colorless lie. An invisible lie. What's an invisible lie? It's one that you tell, and you don't even know it's a lie. It's the lie we tell ourselves—and actually believe! It's the most dangerous of all.

We can keep things from ourselves by lying. We know that we need to change, to drop that habit or address that addiction. But we tell ourselves it's okay. Maybe it's subtle changes in our behavior that we ignore, like how we're letting our anger get to us or how work is really stressing us out. We cover it up and keep it from ourselves. We lie, and we don't even know it.

Or maybe it's something we want to believe, but it's just not true. You don't want to hear that he's just not that into you, so you tell yourself he is. You don't want to know that your job is unfulfilling, so you pretend like it is. If you tell it to yourself long enough, you think it will eventually be true. Call it what it is: self-deception. These invisible lies have just enough of the truth in them to make them believable. Just like the serpent in Eden, who gave Eve just enough truth to get her to bite, we wrap these lies in facts, hoping that enough layers will make the core somehow true. But they don't. And lying to yourself will only keep you stuck.

the true root of false sight

The worst blind spots in our lives are the ones that we think we don't have. You see what you don't want to see, so you pretend it's not there. Or you don't see what you need to see, so you make it up. It's false sight. Seeing what's not true.

We have a blind spot, tell ourselves it's either no big deal or nothing at all, and then find ourselves stuck by some invisible force. It's really that invisible lie. Those invisible lies have a source. They come from the darkness of sin in our lives. The root of false sight is spiritual blindness.

Before we come to have a relationship with God through Jesus, we have no true insight. That's because the Holy Spirit is not in us. Jesus tells us that the Spirit "leads into all truth" (John 14:17). Without that guiding light, we have no way to see ourselves out of that pit. Without the forgiveness of sins, we are left in spiritual darkness. Without a relationship with God, we have no hope of ever recovering our sight. I think the prophet Isaiah perfectly stated what it means to be spiritually blind.

> We grope like the blind along a wall,
> feeling our way like people without eyes.
> Even at brightest noontime,
> we stumble as though it were dark.
> Among the living,
> we are like the dead. (Isaiah 59:10)

Have you ever felt like you were just groping along in life? Like you were running your hands along the side of a wall, not really understanding where you were going? You bump from one relationship to the next. Or you knock into one job after knocking out of the one before it. It's as if you don't even have eyes!

We can go through life with every sign pointing us in the right direction, but we fail to see them. Why? Because without God, we lack true insight. We lack true power. And we lack true life. Have you ever been there? I know I have. It's like being under a spell. In fact, that's exactly what it is. If you think Isaiah's words were harsh, here's what Paul had to say about spiritual blindness: "Satan, who is the god of this world, has blinded the minds of those who don't believe. They are unable to see the glorious light of the Good News. They don't understand this message about the glory of Christ, who is the exact likeness of God" (2 Corinthians 4:4).

Maybe you know someone like this. Their life is on a dead-end track. They're heading for devastation, and they're heading there quick. You've told them about Jesus, but they didn't want to hear. You showed them the love of the gospel, but they refused it. The only thing worse than being stuck is heading straight ahead with no direction.

That directionless life means death. And death comes to our world because of sin (Romans 5:12). We've all sinned. And we share in that same sinful act that knocked Adam and Eve from paradise and set them on a dead-end track.

the two worst feelings in the world

Think back to that story from Genesis 3. Once Adam and Eve ate that fruit, the one fruit God told them not to eat, sin entered the world. And with it, death. Blindness. Spiritual darkness. And everything that comes with those things.

The first thing that happened was that they saw their own nakedness. They were completely exposed. And they felt something they had never, ever experienced before. They felt shame. Up to that point in the history of the world, no one had ever known shame. Now it was all they could feel. Then they heard something, God moving in the garden. They ran and hid! They couldn't be seen by God. Why? They felt something else. The second worst thing to ever be felt on earth. Guilt.

Shame is feeling bad for who you are. Guilt is feeling bad for what you've done. We all feel guilty whenever we do something wrong. At least, we should. If you say something mean to a friend, even if it's careless, you might feel guilty about it. Lying, cheating, stealing all can make you feel guilty. That is a normal reaction. In fact, the Holy Spirit will convict you when you do something wrong. That's one way to look at guilt.

However, when you still feel guilty for something that's already forgiven, that guilt will cloud your vision. You can't see yourself clearly because all you can see are the mistakes you've made. Once you realize that your past sins are under the blood of Christ as a belief, you should walk in freedom from guilt. The answer to feeling guilty about new sins is repentance. Ask for forgiveness and walk in newness. But the answer to feeling guilty for previous, forgiven sins has to come from somewhere deeper.

On the other side of guilt is shame. Adam and Eve felt shame immediately after biting into the forbidden fruit. They weren't ashamed about their sin. That's guilt. They were ashamed of who they were. They saw their nakedness and were filled with disgust. They sewed fig leaves together, but those leaves didn't fit right. They fell apart easily. They did nothing to hide their shame.

Feeling guilty about what you've done is natural. But feeling shame for who you are is not what God intends. When you feel bad about some part of you, the way you look, how you walk, your abilities or lack of them, that's shame. And shame will always hold you back. That's because God made you. He designed you. He carefully constructed you exactly how you are. That's not to say there aren't problems that you need to tackle. But it does mean that you can be confident about yourself at the core.

When you allow shame to lead in your life, it blinds you to the reality of your identity in Christ. Once you come to him, he changes you from who you were to a new creature. Everything changes at the cross, and when we come to the cross, we enter a new process of transformation. We are becoming just like Christ. We are sons and daughters, no longer orphaned. We are servants to God and to righteous living, no longer servants to sin. We are happy and blessed, no longer living under doom and gloom. We are victorious, no longer defeated.

We need to open our eyes and see who we are clearly. We need to overcome the guilt of past sins that holds us down and release ourselves from shame that holds us back. When we do that, we can begin moving forward.

get that out of your eye

I think it's interesting to look carefully at the story of Adam and Eve. They were filled with shame and guilt when they ate the forbidden fruit. But what really changed about them? They didn't go from clothed to naked. They were always naked. God knew it, and they knew it.

So what changed? The way they saw themselves changed. The forbidden fruit, the seed of sin, the beginning of spiritual darkness, clouded their view of themselves. We have all messed up and gotten off track. It's easy to see it in others but really difficult to see it in ourselves. Jesus calls that judging, and he warns us not to do it. When we attack others for their problems but cover up our own, believing our own lies, that can be dangerous. Jesus has a solution: "Why worry about a speck in your friend's eye when you have a log in your own? How can you think of saying to your friend, 'Let me help you get rid of that speck in your eye,' when you can't see past the log in your own eye? Hypocrite! First get rid of the log in your own eye; then you will see well enough to deal with the speck in your friend's eye" (Matthew 7:3–5).

I don't think it's a coincidence that the man in Mark 8 saw people walking around like trees. I think that represents the logs we have in our own eyes. Jesus touched the man, but was he fully healed? No. He had to go through a process. And here in Matthew 7, Jesus was talking to people in relationship with him. These weren't sinners, lost people on the outside. These were insiders. And Jesus told them to remove the trees from their eyes. This man came to Jesus for healing, just like we do when we come to him for salvation. But that healing wasn't immediate and all-encompassing. We want it to be. We want a quick fix. But that second touch from Jesus, the one that cleared his sight fully, is what we all need to strive for.

Maybe you've already made the decision to follow Jesus, but you still have blind spots in your life. Maybe you look at your past through a negative lens. You think you know enough when you only have part of the picture. Or you constantly search for the worst in others, leading with judgment instead of grace. Those things are the result of logs in our eyes.

We all have blind spots, and we should check them regularly. That's why community is so important. Having someone else in your life who can check your blind spots for you is invaluable. The best friend is one who has permission to always be honest. They never tell you a white lie, even when you think you need one. Instead, they can see what you may not be able to and help you identify those blind spots. But without that friend in your life, you're stuck. Or maybe you do have that friend, but you're just ignoring them because you don't want to hear the truth.

God wants us to clean out our eyes. And he wants to help us do that. Spiritual sight is a gift from God. It's not the result of fixing every mistake, erasing every sin, or overcoming every temptation by sheer force of will or habit. It's about leaning into the rest that he has prepared for you and me. When we do that, he will take away our blind spots and help us move forward.

CHAPTER 10

clear your blind spots

Tony Dungy is perhaps the greatest NFL coach of all time. He's definitely in the conversation. He holds a 148–79 record, having been the head coach of the Tampa Bay Buccaneers and the Indianapolis Colts from 1996 to 2008. He won it all with Peyton Manning as quarterback in 2007. And yes, he's in the NFL Hall of Fame.[15]

But it took Coach Dungy a long time to get his first head coaching job. As a standout coordinator on other NFL teams, he interviewed regularly for top openings across the league. But they always turned him down. That is until one team took a chance on his unorthodox coaching philosophy, one that many people attribute to Tampa Bay's Super Bowl victory in 2003, a year after he left.

Normally, coaches teach their teams to read the other team's defense or offense. They come to their position and look at the alignment of the other team. *Who's playing what position? Where are they lined up? Are they getting ready to move to another spot on the field? Here's the snap! Okay, where are the players going?* That type of game plan is pretty standard for football teams. Tony Dungy thought it was terrible. It required the players to memorize so many plays and react in so many different ways over the course of a sixteen-week season. It was inefficient and confusing.

There's a saying in football: "When you see a lot, you see nothing. But when you see one thing, you see everything." Tony Dungy bought into that, and he coached that way too. Instead of having his players memorize plays and charts and patterns, he taught them to focus on just one or two players on the other side of the ball. For instance, a defensive lineman would look at his counterpart on the offensive line. Then, he would focus on where his feet were, how he positioned his hands or shoulders, and where he moved his eyes. Those cues gave the player clues for what type of play was about to happen. *A run play, with the fullback moving to the left—I need to cut him off at the hole. A pass play with the quarterback rolling to his weak side—I need to blitz! It's an option, but the running back is going to be stuck in the backfield. Make like I'm falling for the pass, then attack him at the line.* Focusing on what you are supposed to see rather than trying to see everything all at the same time was the key to success for Tony Dungy and his teams.[16]

But that holds true for us too. What are you seeing in life? What are you looking at? What holds your focus? And what should you see but don't? That's the definition of a blind spot. We all have them. In the last chapter, we looked at how to identify blind spots. Now we need to work on clearing them. Because if we keep focusing on the wrong thing rather than what we truly need to see, we will never get anywhere in life.

blind leading the blind

Do you know where the saying "the blind leading the blind" comes from? If you said Jesus, then you're right! In fact, it's derived almost word for word from Matthew's account of one of Jesus' sermons. "If one blind person guides another, they will both fall into a ditch" (Matthew 15:14). What's worse than having blind spots in your life and getting stuck? It's when your blind spots cause others to get stuck too. That's what Jesus was talking about. And he was talking to a specific group that was spiritually blind. He was pointing out the religious elite.

A religious expert is one who thinks they have it all together. They hear the rules and want to follow every single one. And you know what? They're good at it! At least for a while. They can walk the straight and narrow, they can keep their nose clean, they can obey the rules, and they can keep it all together.

But experts of religion have one major problem. They become excellent judges because they think, *If I can keep it all together, why can't you? What's your problem?* This judgmental attitude doesn't help the people they try to guide. Instead, it keeps them frozen in place.

On the other end of the spectrum are the religious examples. The ones who hear the rules and say, "No way I can do all that. Are you kidding me?" They fail at the law. So they're made examples of that same law. *There's no use trying to follow the rules*, they think. Instead, they fake it as long as possible. They put on a show. It may even be a real show. But eventually it all falls apart. And then they feel completely worthless.

These two ways of thinking, the religious expert and the religious example, are the result of blind spots. They don't understand the truth and purpose of the law. They think it's a standard to live up to. But God knows that we can't live up to that standard. The law, the religious law that is outlined in the Old Testament, was meant to remind us we can't do it on our own. We all need Jesus to do it for us.

Instead of focusing on the one thing, Jesus, they try to focus on everything, the entire law. And they get stuck. It's too much for them. It's too much for anyone! Except for Jesus. We must fix our eyes on him, and he will lead us out. But the religious elite of his time wouldn't hear it. They wanted it their own way. And they suffered blind spots. Their blind spots were so big that they engulfed other people. They didn't know who they really were in God, but they made other people think they did. They got them to follow their example, but they had no clue where they were going.

stuck in the mud just makes you dirty

Do you know what happens when your car gets stuck in the mud? Your tires are spinning. You're going nowhere fast. And you get mud everywhere. Everywhere! Getting stuck in the mud just makes you dirty. Jesus looked at those blind guides, the religious elite, and said, "You're spinning your wheels, and you're getting everyone dirty—including yourself!"

When we fail to clear our blind spots, we can make a mess of our lives and other people's lives. How does that happen? Well, the blind spot itself can be a source of impurity. Many of our own blind spots are places in our lives that we need to allow God to cleanse. But when we don't see them, we don't think they're dirty. The dirt you don't see doesn't bother you.

What's the worst thing you can find in your food at a restaurant? A piece of hair, right? Because it's visible. And it's disgusting. But mostly because it's visible. But drop a cookie on the floor and what do you do? If you're like me, you pick it up. Three-second rule! Which makes no sense because germs don't follow the three-second rule. And the most dangerous, ugly, dirty germs are the ones we can't see. We drop our food, pick it up, brush it off, and think it's clean. But it's not. Let's be honest. We're okay with some dirt as long as we can't see it.

These Pharisees couldn't see their own dirt. They thought they had everything nice and neat in their lives. But they were really quite dirty. Here's what Jesus said about them: "What sorrow awaits you teachers of religious law and you Pharisees. Hypocrites! For you are so careful to clean the outside of the cup and the dish, but inside you are filthy—full of greed and self-indulgence! You blind Pharisee! First wash the inside of the cup and the dish, and then the outside will become clean, too" (Matthew 23:25–26).

Let's say I invite you over to my house for dinner. I'm not sure what I'd make you since I'm not that great of a cook. Can we just agree to order out? Okay, fine. But I'll offer you a nice beverage of your choice! And you get to pick which cup I put it in. For the first cup, I'm going to make sure it's nice and clean. At least on the outside. I'm going to wash and dry it right in front of you. But you'll still be able to see the nasty, dirty, gross inside of that cup. It's filthy. The other cup? Oh, it's kind of dirty too. There are some smudges on it, some blotches on the outside. But it's spotless on the inside. The inside is 100 percent sanitized.

Now which cup do you want your beverage in? Am I right that you said the second one? That's because you know what Jesus knows, that the inside is more important than the outside.

Those religious elites were great at getting their outside world in order. But they were not so good about making sure their inner lives were working right. That's where their blind spots lived. And they didn't care to clear those blind spots.

You may be pretty good at living outwardly like you've got it all together. You may be pretty good at faking it, putting on your Christian face for the world to see. But if you have blind spots within, it won't matter what others think of you. God knows what's in your heart, and he wants to help you out by cleaning up those spots.

inside out

Taking care of those blind spots within our heart actually works to clean up our lives outside as well. That's the irony. If you only work on your outer life, your inner life could suffer. But if you clean up the blind spots of your inner life, God says your outer life will follow.

Let's see if we can find somewhere else in Scripture that talks about this. It won't be too hard. Just do a search for the word *blind.* And here you go, in the words of Peter: "Those who fail to develop in this way are shortsighted or blind, forgetting that they have been cleansed from their old sins" (2 Peter 1:9). And there you have it. Peter was saying that those who don't realize Jesus cleanses us of our sins from inside out are blind, shortsighted. Their blind spots are still there, keeping them stuck. They fail to develop something. What is it? We just have to back up a few verses to see what that whole process is.

> In view of all this, make every effort to respond to God's promises. Supplement your faith with a generous provision of moral excellence, and moral excellence with knowledge, and knowledge with self-control, and self-control with patient endurance, and patient endurance with godliness, and godliness with brotherly affection, and brotherly affection with love for everyone.
>
> The more you grow like this, the more productive and useful you will be in your knowledge of our Lord Jesus Christ. (2 Peter 1:5–8)

This is the process we should go through if we want to clear our blind spots. These are the steps we take once Jesus has forgiven us of our sins. When he begins to cleanse us from the inside out, this is how we know that we are no longer blind, stumbling around, knocking into each other. Peter taught us about seven steps. Let's take these one at a time.

1. apply his promises to your life

"Make every effort to respond to God's promises…"

God has promised you so much. It begins with his promise to save you, to forgive your sins, to cleanse you, and to make you righteous. We begin to clear our blind spots when we embrace his promises in our lives.

What promise has he given you that you haven't seen realized yet? Keep on believing him for it. He will stand by it if you move out in it. We get stuck when we stop looking to him for his promises. Don't let your wheels keep spinning. Lean into his promises today.

2. live a good life

"Supplement your faith with a generous provision of moral excellence..."

Now Peter gives us some rapid-fire promises that go from one to the other, each building on the one before it. Here, he uses the word *supplement*. I like that word a lot. Supplements are what you take when you're really into exercise and bodybuilding. When you're putting in the work, those supplements kick in and help grow you from the inside out.

The first supplement is to just live a good life. Moral excellence is how Peter puts it. I think morality is a lost concept in the world today. People are so concerned with what they're getting that they're not worried about how they're living. We need to see clearly that our actions have consequences. When you commit to living a good life, you never have to worry about bad consequences. What area of your life needs the most work right now? You're leaning into God's promises, but are you backing that up with right action? It's all about living out the righteousness he promised to plant inside you. Let it grow, and you will soon find yourself making good decisions.

3. get to know God better

"...and knowledge..."

As you continue to apply those promises to your life, the knowledge God placed within you will produce more and more growth. This is what the Holy Spirit does; it helps us know God better. When we lean into the rest God has provided, it's for a purpose. That purpose is not to clean up your theology or clear up your doctrine. It's not to make you a smarter Bible reader. It's to help you know God better.

What's more important to you than knowing God? Paul said there was nothing more valuable for him than the honor of getting to know his Lord: "Yes, everything else is worthless when compared with the infinite value of knowing Christ Jesus my Lord. For his sake I have discarded everything else, counting it all as garbage, so that I could gain Christ" (Philippians 3:8). Can you say the same thing? Or do you need to reprioritize your life so you are getting to know him better?

4. show some self-control

"...and self-control..."

Now is when these supplements start to kick into high gear. You're making good decisions and getting to know God, but before you know it, temptations are going to hit you. How are you going to deal with them? Are you sure your will power is enough? It hasn't been much help so far. Godly self-control is not about us being perfect. It's about us perfectly following the voice of God in every decision of our life.

When was the last time you really messed up? Do you wish you could have a do-over? The good news is that God is the God of do-overs. He loves to forgive people. But he also loves to help you stay in control and resist every temptation. Are you ready?

5. practice patience and endurance

"...and patient endurance..."

Now that we're really moving and cleaning out those blind spots, we have to learn how to wait on God. Sometimes we jump at the chance to be part of the religious elite because they promise real results really fast. But they are just offering false hope with a quick fall. Instead, stick to God's promises on God's time.

Are you tired of waiting? That's normal. But when you are full of the Holy Spirit, you can be patient about anything. You can endure any hardship. You can overcome any circumstance. When you clear out your blind spots, you start to see God's plan take shape. It may not happen at the rate you want it to, but God in his wisdom is working all things for your good.

6. grow in goodness

"...and godliness..."

This is a little different from just making good decisions and living a good life. Most of that is about avoiding bad decisions. This has at its root the idea that service is a way to get closer to God. When you allow service to find a root within you, your blind spots start to melt away.

How do you serve someone each day? Do you automatically want to help meet a need? Or do you need God to help you see it that way? Serving others doesn't hold us back; instead, it propels us forward. If you are only serving yourself, you'll get stuck. So find a way to show some godly goodness right now.

7. love each other

"...and brotherly affection with love for everyone."

I think this is the final result of clearing out your blind spots. Too often those blind areas keep us focused on ourselves. Sure, we can serve others. But why? It may be to try to get something out of it. Or it may just be blind obedience. When you knock off that last blind spot, you not only see yourself differently, but you also see others differently. You see them for who they are. And you love them for who they are.

Who are you loving today? It's easy to love those who love you back. But what about your enemies? Jesus told us to love our neighbor, and that's hard enough. But when Peter said for us to show "love for everyone," he left out no one.

We can do these things all on our own, trying to get better and clearing those blind spots through our own willpower. Or we can lean on Jesus' power, letting him do what he's always wanted to do for us. The first way will either make us religious experts or religious examples. But doing it the second way frees us from religious elitism and instead keeps us moving forward in Christ.

CHAPTER 11

activate your strengths

"Whatcha got under the hood?"

Have you ever been asked that question? It's about your car's engine. Whoever is asking wants to know how big or powerful or how many cams or whatever your engine has. That's what that question is all about.

If you've ever been asked that question and could answer without consulting your car's user guide, then you're what we call a gearhead. I'm not. I've never really known what I have under the hood. It's an engine. I know it's a gas engine. I just push the pedal, and it goes forward unless I put it in reverse. If that's the case, I better check my mirrors. I can tell you how many mirrors I have on my car. That's more important to me than what type of engine I have. Because if I'm not checking my rearview mirrors, I might get into an accident, and my insurance rates will go up. I like the question, "What kind of insurance rates do you have on your car?" That one is more relevant to my life.

But all of us need to know the answer to the question, "Whatcha got under the hood?" when it has to do with our life. What's inside you? Do you know? You should. Because what's inside will always come out.

your inside power

Do you ever read the stories of miracles in the book of Acts and wonder why they don't happen as often today? I know miracles still work. I believe in a miracle-working God. And I realize that there are still places here on earth where miracles happen every day.

But it seems to me that there is a sort of disconnect with the anticipation of those first Christians. They didn't just believe God could do something miraculous; they also expected it to happen. They put themselves in position for it to happen. Look no further than the second story of Acts. After Luke related the story of the coming of the Holy Spirit on the day of Pentecost, he immediately followed it with a story of Peter and John going to the temple.

There was a man there who couldn't walk. He didn't want a miracle; he just asked for money. But Peter said, "I don't have any silver or gold for you. But I'll give you what I have" (Acts 3:6). Then he reached his hand out, he helped the man up, and the man was healed. Instantly! Miraculously! Unmistakably by the power of the Holy Spirit.

What was inside Peter had to come out. He began telling anyone who would listen in the temple grounds that Jesus had done this. Peter explained that the power inside him was not his own, but it was from God. And over five thousand people heard him and turned to faith. In Acts 4:4 it says, "Many of the people who heard their message believed it, so the number of men who believed now totaled about 5,000." You and I can read that and think, *Wow, I wish that would happen in my church.* I pray that it does! But one reason we don't see it as often, I think, is what happened next in the story.

While Peter and John were speaking to the people, the priests, the captain of the temple guard, and some of the Sadducees confronted them. These leaders were very disturbed that Peter and John were teaching the people that through Jesus there is a resurrection of the dead (4:1–2). They were disturbed that Peter and John were talking about Jesus. Disturbed that they were giving credit for a miracle to a man whom, just a couple of months before, these same leaders had condemned to die. Disturbed that this man, Jesus, was still stirring in the hearts of his followers. They were not just disturbed though. They were downright hostile. They grabbed Peter and John and threw them in the temple jail.

In Acts 4, you read about the first flickers of persecution that would soon turn into a raging fire. Peter and John were called in front of the Sanhedrin, the religious ruling class of the day, and were raked over the coals. Imagine that! You see a lame person walk, and your first reaction is to criticize.

But how many of us are so afraid of criticism, of persecution, of humiliation that we stop short. We don't press into what God put inside us. Instead, we stay silent, ready to proclaim Jesus in church but not wanting to make a big deal about it in the world. I'm afraid that our unwillingness to face that criticism means we keep what's inside locked up tight. But the truth is that what is inside you has to come out. If you are a follower of Jesus, then the Holy Spirit has taken up residence inside you. And he wants to come out of you. Let's take a closer look at what it means to live an inside-out life.

what goes in must come out

Here's what I know to be absolutely true. Anything you put inside you will, at some time in the future, come out of you. And I mean anything. But don't take my word for it. Jesus said the same thing. There was another time, earlier in Jesus' ministry, when these same Pharisees and religious leaders got really mad at him. Why? Because he and his followers weren't washing their hands the right way.

You and I make sure to wash our hands in the restroom, right? Well, there's one way to wash them, and then there's the religious way to wash them. And Jesus and his disciples didn't follow the religious way to the letter. So the Pharisees got mad. They even accused them of being dirty. But Jesus said, "Can't you see that the food you put into your body cannot defile you? Food doesn't go into your heart, but only passes through the stomach and then goes into the sewer" (Mark 7:18–19). See, I told you Jesus said it. Then Jesus said this: "It is what comes from inside that defiles you" (v. 20). Why? Because what is inside you will come out of you.

So what are you putting inside yourself? Not what are you eating, but what are you putting into your heart? You will only get out what you put in. I love the character Jason Bourne from the Robert Ludlum novels and the film series. He's pretty much my hero. He's like James Bond but Americanized. In other words, super cool. He's the only guy in movies who can use a magazine to fight off multiple terrorists or rig a bomb with a paperclip and a table fan.

If I got to choose who I wanted to be in life, I would have chosen to be Jason Bourne. But I can't because I don't get to choose, for one. But also because I don't have it in me. I don't have the training and skill and physical makeup for it. I don't have it in me to run flat out for half a mile before my hands start shaking. I can get about a block, maybe half a block. I can't be Jason Bourne because I don't have what Jason Bourne has in him. The only thing we really have in common is that we are both from small towns in Missouri.

I am a product of what I put inside me. That's why I must be careful what goes inside me, into my heart. We all better have a good idea of what is inside us. How does it get there? Jesus said it's not through our mouth: "It's not what goes into your body that defiles you; you are defiled by what comes from your heart" (Mark 7:15). What comes from our heart gets there through our ears and our eyes mostly. If I constantly listen to music full of cussing and bad messages, guess what's going to come out of me. If I'm watching movies about gore and death, guess what's going to come out of me. If I'm reading things that are hateful and hurtful, guess what's going to come out of me.

But if I'm listening to godly music, reading his Word often, and surrounding myself with positive messages of love, I can guarantee you that I won't have a problem with what comes out of me. I'm not going to doubt that my words will be gracious and godly. I won't worry that I might respond to someone with anger or hate. If, that is, I'm doing those things consistently. But it's not just that. We need a clear view of who we are in Christ, how he has made us, how he is redeeming us, if we are ever going to activate those strengths. That includes things like your education or even lack of it. I'm not saying education isn't important, but not having a formal degree can't stop the Holy Spirit in you.

What about your specific heritage or ethnicity? Have you ever thought about how your experience growing up may place you in a unique position to offer strength and hope to others? Instead of viewing our circumstances as roadblocks, ask God to show you what he's put in you to overcome them—and then help others activate their own strengths.

Your talent, your skill set, your work experience, your career choice, even your passions and hobbies. God is using all those things to deposit strength within, little by little. When you follow Jesus, all of your life is baptized in his purposes. And all of it can be used for his mission in your life. You may not be Jason Bourne, but that doesn't mean you can't be the best possible you.

Peter was like Jason Bourne though. Think about it. He had the same boldness to stand up to authority. He broke out of jail. He was a world traveler. Sometimes he even went undercover. So what did Peter have that I don't or you don't? Or what did he have that we do, but we just haven't realized it yet? That's the real question. We need to understand what he had been putting inside his heart to see how those things came out of him. In fact, that's exactly what the religious leaders asked Peter. "They brought in the two disciples and demanded, 'By what power, or in whose name, have you done this?'" (Acts 4:7).

haters gonna hate

Peter and John and the rest of the disciples were Jews, just like these religious leaders. In other words, they were all coming from the same perspective. At least they should have been, given their early Torah training. The only difference is that Peter and John and the other disciples believed that Jesus was the promised Messiah. And when they did that, it was too much for those religious leaders. They couldn't believe; at least, a lot of them didn't. The ones who didn't were so upset, so filled with hate toward these Jesus followers, that it makes you wonder what was in their hearts the whole time.

But the point I want you to get is this. Peter and John were not persecuted by those whom they didn't know. They were persecuted by their friends. They were persecuted by family members. They faced all sorts of opposition from within, those who surrounded them, those whom they thought they could trust. And if you think that might not be the case for you, take another look. It is nearly impossible to do ministry today without being online. For me, that comes with a fair share of online trolls. People I was formerly close with have left vulgar comments on my sermons, including on the church's website. Obviously I delete them as soon as I spot them. I process this by believing it's an attack from the Enemy, and I hold Satan responsible while still maintaining compassion for the people who posted the comments.

At one point, even a fellow pastor was offering negative criticisms on my sermon. Not only that, but he also sent the worship pastor at the church I was pastoring a very long message detailing all the shortcomings in my sermons. He was urging the worship pastor to share his critiques with our leader board. I know I'm not the perfect preacher, but that's taking things a little too far. After all, we have a local elder board and an entire congregation that can help gauge the effectiveness of my sermons. It turns out that this pastor was holding on to some jealousy toward me. He was upset that he wasn't considered for a position that I was offered at a previous church.

People will surprise you. There will always be people, even those closest to you, who will try to tear you down on your way to your destiny. Because haters gonna hate. It's what they do. Those you think you can trust may not be as trustworthy as you want them to be. And it can be devastating to your dream.

There were two words that Luke, the author of Acts, used in describing how these religious leaders hated on Peter and John: *demand* and *power*. They demanded that the apostles explain to them whose power they were using.

Haters will always demand things from you. They will demand their own way, their own opinion of you, and their own desires over your God-given dreams. Real friends don't demand; they dig. They want to know what's inside you because they are just so amazed at what they're seeing come out of you. They will dig deep and find a way to help you live out that dream.

Haters are always obsessed with power. They say things like, "Who do you think you are?" They try to knock your dream down a notch. Why? Because they usually lack any power inside. The ones who are the loudest in their criticism are usually the most insecure in their own strength and dreams.

Instead of listening to the demands for power, we need to locate the power God has already placed inside us. If you are a true follower of Jesus, then you don't need to present any credentials. You only need to find that spark within and let it work its way out of you.

show me what you're made of

Did you see the movie *Black Panther*? I hope you did! It was one of the best stories of integrity and perseverance while finding a way to victory. During a pivotal part at the beginning of the movie, T'Challa, the heir to the title of Black Panther, must fend off a challenge from M'Baku, a member of another tribe. Just when you think M'Baku is going to win, the queen mother lets out a cry. "Show him who you are!"[17]

That's the type of sentence that can change your life. I got so excited when I heard it that I nearly jumped out of my seat. I don't know if anyone else in the theater would have minded though. We might have started a church right then.

Do you know who you are? If you do, then show us! If you've put in the work to find and clear your blind spots, if you've spent the energy to work through the problem of your circumstances, if you've committed to consistently relying on God's rest, then you surely know who you are! And that's when it's time to show the haters, the critics, the doubters, and the fence-sitters just who you are. That's what Peter did.

> Peter, filled with the Holy Spirit, said to them, "Rulers and elders of our people, are we being questioned today because we've done a good deed for a crippled man? Do you want to know how he was healed? Let me clearly state to all of you and to all the people of Israel that he was healed by the powerful name of Jesus Christ the Nazarene, the man you crucified but whom God raised from the dead…There is salvation in no one else! God has given no other name under heaven by which we must be saved." (Acts 4:8–10, 12)

Peter said, "You want to know whose authority we are working under? You want to know about the power we have? You want us to give you a name? Okay, here it is—Jesus!" Peter got really theological on them and decided to point some blame while he was at it. I can just picture him pointing his finger at all of them when he said, "Jesus Christ the Nazarene, the man you crucified but whom God raised from the dead."

The haters thought they had stopped Jesus, but God raised him from the dead. The religious leaders thought they had shut Peter up, but the Holy Spirit filled him with power. You might think that your dream has come up short. But I want you to know that if Jesus is in you, then power will come out of you. All you have to do is activate those strengths.

shut your mouth!

What do you think happened when Peter gave them a little look at what he was made of? "There was nothing the council could say" (Acts 4:14). The Holy Spirit had healed a man, Jesus had been declared, and God had been glorified. The haters had to shut up.

These religious leaders were paid to speak. That was their whole job: to sit at this big table and make declarations, telling others what to do. But when their criticism met the strength of God's dream activated within Peter, they were left completely useless.

What was it that shut them up? Luke told us that three things stopped these guys in their tracks. First, they saw the boldness of Peter and John. It's amazing what happens when we let our faith show. Confidence in God is something others will be able to recognize in you.

In a grade school science class, I learned about the different types of energy. I'm sure there are more, but the two that really stuck out to me were potential and kinetic energy. An example of potential energy is when you put a rubber band on your finger and pull it back nice and tight. It's full of potential! Kinetic energy is when you let it fly.

Here's what I remember about potential and kinetic energy. They are directly related. The more potential energy you have, the more kinetic energy you'll get. The farther you pull that rubber band back, the farther it will fly. The more you put in, the more you'll get out.

Our boldness is directly related to the faith we put in the Holy Spirit within us. If we truly believe that God can do it, then he will. If we dream big dreams, then we will have great boldness. It's all about making sure that deposit has as much potential energy as we can get down in there. And when we let it out, it has the power to shut the mouths of every critic.

Ashley was a young leader in whom I saw a lot of potential. She was an excellent volunteer and always showed up on time. However, she was a bit timid and pretty quiet. I asked her to volunteer to take over the small groups for our student ministry. When I shared my decision with my church leadership, a few of them actually laughed aloud. They begged me to recant my decision and place someone else in that role, not believing that Ashley had what it took. I doubled down on the choice, knowing I was placing my own validity as a leader on the line.

There was never a doubt in my mind that Ashley would go above and beyond to accomplish our ministry goals with excellence. Soon our small groups blew up, and almost 100 percent of our students were attending one. She organized curriculum, scheduled volunteers, and found new group leaders. Because of her active energy, there were more teenagers than adults in small groups in our church of over twelve hundred people.

Soon after, the executive leaders of the church noticed what I already had. They offered her a staff position at the church. A few years later, the denomination asked her to lead the kids' ministry for the entire movement at their largest annual event. She was full of potential energy that needed a kick start to move into her kinetic destiny.

The next thing that Luke told us is that Peter and John were just ordinary people. These leaders didn't see anything great—no degree from an Ivy League school, no huge bank account, no name up in lights. Just two guys who were fisherman. Their clothes might still have carried a bit of old herring odor.

But there's more to this than you might think. That's a pretty simple detail in Acts 4:13, that they had no special training, but they had been with Jesus. You see, in those days, every young Jewish boy was raised to learn the Torah. That's the first five books of the Bible. And when I say learn, I mean memorize. Word for word. That education went on until age ten. At that time, most boys would then go on to learn the family business, like fishing. Keep that in mind. But there were a select few who would continue studying Scripture and the Law. Part of that advanced education included memorizing all the Hebrew Scriptures, what you and I call the Old Testament, from Genesis to Malachi. All of it. Every single word, memorized.

With that accomplished, which would take a few years, these boys would then want to be selected by a rabbi for even more training. To become a disciple. That meant they would literally sit at the feet of a teacher, learn from them what the Scriptures mean, and one day gain their own authority and become rabbis themselves.

But it wasn't an automatic application. You had to wait. And wait and wait and wait sometimes. You had to be ready for a rabbi to notice you and call you. They would say, "Come, follow me." Sound familiar? The boys the rabbis chose were always the best of the best, the top of the class. If a rabbi didn't choose you, you were left out. You went back home, and you learned the family trade. Like fishing. Like Peter and John did.

All indications are that Peter and John had completed their initial training in Judaism, learning the Torah, and had even advanced to the next level. But they were left off. They didn't make the cut. Until the day Jesus walked along the edge of the water and saw them fishing, working in the family business. And he said, "Come, follow me." No wonder they were so eager to drop their nets! It was unheard of for a rabbi to call an adult male to follow him. Their time was up; their chance was over. But Peter and John and their brothers also were different. Why? Because Jesus saw something in them that no one else did. Not their instructors. Not the other rabbis. And certainly not these religious leaders. That is, until Peter and John opened their mouths and proved them wrong.

You and I don't need to wait for a big name, enough money, or an advanced degree. We have all we need in our ordinary lives to do something extraordinary for God. You and I don't need to be rocket scientists. You and I don't need to be movie stars. You and I don't need to be president. We just need to be who God says we are. It all comes down to what's inside.

The last thing that Luke made sure we know is that these religious leaders saw these two guys and knew they had been with Jesus. Imagine that! Just by looking at them they could tell these were the type who had spent time with a rabbi from Galilee, a martyr hung on a cross, a Messiah risen from the grave. I hope that others see that in me. Every day when I spend time with Jesus, I want to be able to walk away with a certain something around me that lets everyone know I've been with Jesus. Not to brag but to confirm that what's inside me is ready to burst out.

Resting in God's presence will result in action. It's what creates potential energy in your life. It's what produces great dreams that you can't help but follow through with. If we really want to see God do some amazing, Holy Spirit–led, first-chapters-of-Acts-type miracle stuff, it's going to take spending time resting in Jesus' presence. Are you ready?

we just can't stop

Many men tried to stop Jesus' movement. Give them credit; they did whatever they could do. They jailed the disciples, beat them, even stoned some of them. But they just couldn't stop them. Why? Because once Peter activated his strengths, there was no turning back. This is his response to these religious leaders' demands that the disciples should never talk about Jesus again: "We cannot stop telling about everything we have seen and heard" (Acts 4:20).

When you activate your strengths, you just can't stop. It will come out of you. That was the point Peter and James were making. Trying to stop it is like trying to stop breathing. You breathe in, and you breathe out. What's inside will come out, no matter what. The only way you can stop it is if you stop breathing. So as long as we have breath in our lungs, let's keep activating our strengths. Let's find out what God has put inside us, and let's find ways to get it out of us.

If you are not sure what your strengths are, take a test like StrengthsFinder by Gallup or a spiritual gifts inventory to have more clarity. Keep those in mind as you continue to the next section of this book.

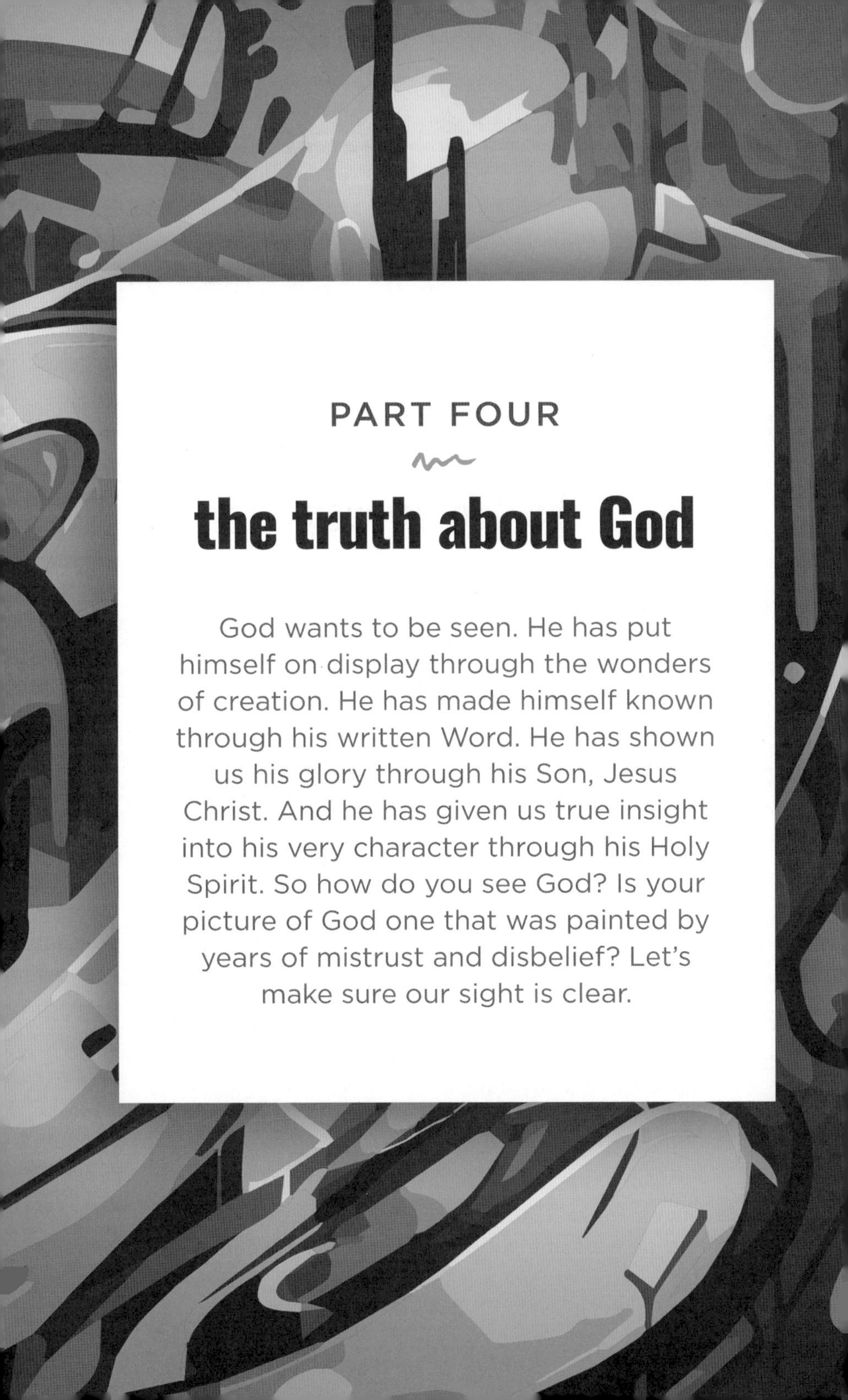

PART FOUR

the truth about God

God wants to be seen. He has put himself on display through the wonders of creation. He has made himself known through his written Word. He has shown us his glory through his Son, Jesus Christ. And he has given us true insight into his very character through his Holy Spirit. So how do you see God? Is your picture of God one that was painted by years of mistrust and disbelief? Let's make sure our sight is clear.

CHAPTER 12

the God we need

In order to see who God is, we sometimes have to settle ourselves with who he isn't. It's not enough to learn new things about him; we also have to clear out the old clutter.

First of all, God is not a genie in the sky granting every one of your wishes. Don't you sometimes wish he were though? But that's how some of us treat God. We take him for granted until we really need something. We hold off talking to him until it's urgent. We stop communicating with him until we're through making our list. "Okay, God, I'm ready. Here's my list. Can I get this by Wednesday?"

But God is not a genie in the sky, a personal wish granter for the chosen few. That would mean he is your servant. That would put the relationship in reverse, flip-flopped, upside down. When we see God as a genie in the sky, we assume that he's beneath us. That he is inferior to our desires. Instead, our desires should be inferior to his glory.

The other way we get it wrong is by thinking of him as a disappointed dad. Arms folded, head wagging back and forth. It's not so much that he's mad at us, but boy, could we have done a lot better than that. The beginning truth of the gospel message is that we have all sinned (Romans 3:23). We have messed up, missed the mark, and made huge mistakes. There's no denying that. But seeing God in the same light as an authoritarian figure you've ticked off won't help your situation.

God is not mad at you. He does not hate you. He is not disappointed in you. He loves you. He knows what you did, for he saw all of it. He watched as you began to step off the rails and head toward that bad decision. And he knew what was just ahead for you—heartache, pain, regret, guilt. But God's love outweighs our sin. You cannot imagine the cost he paid to clean up your mess. When we see him as a disappointed dad, we misunderstand his love for us. It's not a stern, cold, calculated love. It's not the tough love you might have experienced growing up. It's warm and caring. It's unconditional.

If you look at it a different way, when we view God as a genie, we are always asking, "Why doesn't God see me?" We're waving our hands, hoping he sees us so he can give us whatever we want. And when we view him as a disappointed dad? Well, it goes the other way. We hope he doesn't see us at all. We're hiding, just like Adam and Eve in the garden.

Both those misperceptions of God have one thing in common. They assume that God is way up there, looking down on us. He's either holding his hands just waiting for our command to follow or putting them on his hips and hoping you don't mess up. Either way, he's the far-off God. I would hate to worship a god who was far away. There's no feeling of warmth, no reassurance. He can't really hear us because the distance is too great. He can't really guide us because our eyes are too weak. So we just sit and stay.

But God is not a far-off god. He is always right there. Paul told us that God is not way up in heaven, so far that we can't get to him, or way down below the earth, so deep we can't find him. Instead, he's "close at hand" (Romans 10:8). He's right beside you if you dare to believe it.

When we see God as the genie in the sky or the disappointed dad, we put our desires or our fears in front of him. Like blocking out all light by putting our hands in front of our face, when we try to move, we trip and fall or hit the wall. So instead, we just stay perfectly still. But God wants you to move out and move forward. So we need to take the blinders off and see who he really is.

a long walk with an old friend

Two guys were traveling from Jerusalem to Emmaus three days after Jesus' crucifixion. They heard some rumors that Jesus had risen from the dead. That the tomb didn't hold him, the Roman guards couldn't stop him, and the grave couldn't contain him. But they weren't sure.

It's seven long miles from Jerusalem to Emmaus, and by foot along dusty Palestinian roads, it can take all day. People were likely to encounter others making the journey, and these two did just that. Soon another man walked up on them. These two must have been engrossed in their conversation because this man said, "What are you discussing so intently as you walk along?" (Luke 24:17).

They shared with him what they had heard. Well, this was new information to this man. Or at least he pretended it was. But to the two men's surprise, he began to show them, line by line, how all of it made sense if they just read the Old Testament. They were shocked!

Once they got to their home, they invited the man in. He said he needed to keep traveling, but they finally convinced him to at least share a meal. "As they sat down to eat, he took the bread and blessed it. Then he broke it and gave it to them. Suddenly, their eyes were opened, and they recognized him" (vv. 30–31).

Who was this man? I'm sure you've figured it out by now. It was Jesus, the one who had just risen from the dead.

Now put yourself back in that day. The governor, Pontius Pilate, was going crazy, wondering how the guards could have fallen asleep and let someone roll the rock away from the tomb.

The Jewish leaders were worried. If these reports were right, then they were in serious trouble. And the disciples were cautiously excited. Could it be true? Did Mary really see Jesus in the garden? Did Peter and John actually walk into an empty tomb?

So this Son of God, Jesus Christ, the Messiah, risen from the dead on the first Easter—if he were a far-off god, he would use some huge announcement, some big-scale event, some spectacular display to let everyone know. Maybe he'd strike all his enemies dead at night. Or perhaps he would blast the news through the air, painting it on the sky.

Instead, he took a walk. It's really interesting what Jesus did that first day out of the grave. First, he found some friends. He just decided to start walking next to these guys who had followed him for about three years. That's how he wants to show up in our lives. He wants to walk next to us. He places himself beside us. Whenever we want to encounter God, we can just turn our head. He's right there.

What else did he do? He struck up a conversation. Sure, it's a pretty important one. It's a great biblical and theological explanation about the risen Messiah. But you know what? It was what they wanted to talk about. He doesn't always set the agenda. Sometimes he just wants to hear from us.

Finally, and this is where it gets really good, he sat down and ate with them. That's it! He just wants to have a meal with us. Sometimes the most spiritual thing we can do is have a snack with Jesus. And get this—as soon as he broke that bread, they got it! They saw exactly who he was. Because they'd seen this before. This was exactly who Jesus had been to them for so long. Don't you want to be one of those who gets it, who understands who he is? Who sits down and from the first bite is plugged into who God is?

the most unlikely?

You might have a basic idea of God, sort of a fuzzy picture of him. You know enough to call yourself a Christian, but you couldn't pass a theology test. That's for those other people in the Bible. The real pillars of faith, the founders of religion.

What if I told you someone in the Bible without those credentials saw God clearly and understood him completely? Someone who was an outcast, a nobody, a nothing, but who met God and was changed into a real somebody?

Go back to the first book of the Bible with me. There you'll find stories about Abraham, a man whom we know as the founder of the Jewish faith. God made a covenant with him and told him he would be the father of many nations. But Abraham—he used to be called just Abram—had a problem. His wife, Sarah—who used to be called Sarai—was barren. They had tried for years and years but no baby. Finally, Sarai had a plan. It was not a great plan. But she was desperate to make Abraham happy.

"Now Sarai, Abram's wife, had not been able to bear children for him. But she had an Egyptian servant named Hagar. So Sarai said to Abram…'Go and sleep with my servant. Perhaps I can have children through her.' And Abram agreed with Sarai's proposal" (Genesis 16:1–2). In the next verse we learn that it had been ten years since God had given Abram the promise to make of him a great nation. Ten long years. And nothing to show for it. They were both getting older.

Soon after God called them to leave their home and travel to Canaan, Abram and Sarai found themselves in Egypt during a famine. We can only assume that it was there where Hagar joined them. It makes sense. Abram had lots of livestock and hired hands. Sarai oversaw feeding a whole troop. She needed help, and Hagar checked all the right boxes.

But now imagine it from Hagar's perspective. Picture her standing in the middle of a square in the Egyptian capital. How old was she? Perhaps as young as four or five. Maybe a little older. Where were her parents? Were they enslaved themselves? Or perhaps she was an orphan, part of a conquered people from a war the mighty Egyptians won easily. Regardless, she was there that day when Abram and Sarai walked through the marketplace. Perhaps Abram was only wanting to buy some goods for the long trip back to Canaan, but something caught Sarai's eye. Or better yet, someone caught her eye.

The auctioneer began to call out for bids, and men stood around wagering how much this young girl would bring. What's her name? Hagar? Never mind, she'll do fine. Sarai nudged Abram's side, and he raised a hand to bid. He called out again and again, outbidding all the rest. She would be perfect, Sarai explained. And Abram was willing to pay any price. He was, after all, rich beyond measure and blessed beyond belief.

Sarai and Abram would treat Hagar well. There's no doubt about that. But that doesn't deny the fact that the auctioneer only saw her as a product, and Abram only saw her as a purchase. No one would look at her as a person. Not yet, at least. Fast-forward a decade or so, and Abram, Sarai, and Hagar were now in a difficult predicament. You see, Sarai's plan worked. Hagar was pregnant. But I don't have to tell you there was some drama. Hagar finally had the upper hand over her mistress. After playing the role of slave for so long, she wanted to be seen as equal to Sarai. She even started to think of herself as better than her boss. After all, she was pregnant.

This triangle came to a head when Sarai complained one too many times to Abram about it. "Abram replied, 'Look, she is your servant, so deal with her as you see fit.' Then Sarai treated Hagar so harshly that she finally ran away" (Genesis 16:6).

Now poor Hagar, pregnant and all alone, sneaked out of her tent in the middle of the night. Only able to grab a few things to take with her, she walked through the dark until dawn. That was when she realized she was in trouble. She was on her way to Shur, a little outpost in one of the worst deserts. So in other words, she was halfway to the middle of nowhere.

Hagar was all alone. Or at least she thought she was. Then she heard a voice. It was God speaking through his angel, calling out to this slave girl, this outsider. She was not part of the covenant. But the God of the covenant gets to decide whom he shows up for. God, through an angel, called Hagar's name and got her attention. I wonder how many times Sarai or Abram called her by name. I wonder if they would always just say, "Hey, you," to her.

But God knew her name. And he spoke to her words of promise and hope when she was all out of both. "Return to your mistress, and submit to her authority…I will give you more descendants than you can count" (vv. 9–10).

Hagar must have wondered if it was wise to go back to such a bad situation. But the angel reassured her. "You are now pregnant and will give birth to a son. You are to name him Ishmael (which means 'God hears'), for the Lord has heard your cry of distress" (v. 11).

And then Hagar did something amazing. This is so incredible that she was the first person in the Bible to do it. She gave God a name. Think about that for a second. Her master, Abram, never gave God a name. Noah? The one who was faithful through the flood? He didn't either. Go all the way back to Adam, in his perfect innocence, who was great at giving names—he named all the animals! But one thing he never did was call God by a name. But here is this Egyptian slave, running away from the only home she had known for at least a decade, who encountered the God of the universe and gave him a name: she called him *El-Roi* (v. 13).

Hagar grew up surrounded by Egyptian religion. And the Egyptians worshiped gods, plural. A lot of gods. Each one had its own power, its own little part of nature it oversaw. Hagar would have known each one's name. She would have learned about their stories and their significance. But she never really knew them, never met them. Not like she had the one true God.

There was Horus, the god of the sky and sun. But he was too high in the air ruling the day to notice Hagar. Then there was Hopi, the god of the great Nile River. But he was too quick, rushing down the mighty currents, to stop and see Hagar. Don't forget Isis, the mother goddess of all Egypt. But she was too busy overseeing the other gods to pay attention to Hagar.

But when Hagar met this God, the one true God, she didn't know his name. She knew the names of every impersonal god she worshiped as a young child. But now? She was left without any marker to remember him. She needed to remember this moment. She cried out, naming the God who rescued her, who met her, who finally paid attention to her.

"El-Roi." That sort of sounds funny. Until you know what it means. *El* means "God," and *roi* means "see." "You are the God who sees me," she cried out (Genesis 16:13).

the God you don't need

We don't need a wish-granting genie-god or a head-shaking, disappointed dad-god. We don't need a god who is way up there and doesn't notice us. We need an intimate relationship with the real God. Here's what Hagar realized after her own intimate encounter with that God: "Have I truly seen the One who sees me?" (v. 13).

Intimacy is scary. It means that we reveal all of us. It can set us up for failure. What if the other person rejects us? So we freeze up and can't move forward. In relationships, in our jobs, at church. We'd rather sit on the sidelines and keep to ourselves. If we don't get serious, we can't get hurt again. There are days when we'd rather have a genie-god or a disappointed dad-god. Those pictures are easier to take. They're easier to look at. When we see God for who he isn't, we don't have to deal with who we are. The God who sees us? We'd rather not see him.

But being resilient will require us to move into intimacy again. Whether we know it or not, sticking to that inaccurate picture of God will only keep us stuck. It will keep us frozen. That's because neither of those images have much power in them. They don't really have a chance to help us move past our mistakes, beyond our failures, and into future success.

But an intimate relationship with a God who is close at hand? One who sees us and whom we can see? That's when we can really get moving. Once we open up, let God know us fully and know him fully, we realize he is a great promise keeper. He is pretty bad at rejection. He doesn't know how to reject you! That's because he's committed to you.

When I was in high school, I attended a summer church camp. During one of the worship experiences at an evening service, the presence of God powerfully fell. Dozens of students were at the altar praying and crying for hours. I stayed over to the side of the room by myself. God allowed me to have an encounter with him that was so real that I was confused about how it was even possible.

Either through a vision or in my mind's eye, I was standing with Jesus. We had a conversation about the heavy weights I had been carrying around. Even as I stood there with Jesus, my shoulders were slumped, and my back was hunched due to the pressure of what I was feeling. Then Jesus held up a black trash bag. He asked me to begin to put into that bag everything I was carrying. One by one, I lifted off some of my struggles like anxiety, fear, and anger, handing them to Jesus. He delicately handled each one, placing them into the bag. When I was finished, he tied the bag shut and said, "These are mine to carry now." I was standing up straight and confident. Jesus was smiling. It was a personal encounter with a big God.

It reminded me of this Scripture passage: "Jesus said, 'Come to me, all of you who are weary and carry heavy burdens, and I will give you rest. Take my yoke upon you. Let me teach you, because I am humble and gentle at heart, and you will find rest for your souls. For my yoke is easy to bear, and the burden I give you is light'" (Matthew 11:28–30). God is a powerful God, but his greatest strength is in his intimate and committed love for us.

Hagar didn't need a god who controlled the sun and sky, but she encountered the God who created both. She didn't need a god who rode the Nile, but she met the God who causes the rivers to flow. She didn't need a goddess mother, but she met the God who was closer than her own parents. Hagar in that moment needed someone to see her. And God did.

Sometimes we don't need a God who controls the weather, turns the tides, moves the planets—even though we have that in our God. Sometimes we don't need a God who thunders from heaven and powers the world—even though it's the same God we're looking for. Sometimes we just need a God who sees us. And whom we can see.

What do you see when you see God? It really depends on what you're looking for. When you see God for who he is, you can move from stuck to success.

CHAPTER 13

who God is

Jesus was a great theology teacher. Anyone could pass his class with flying colors. He didn't use big, complicated words. And he never made people memorize long, detailed doctrine. Instead, he told stories. He painted pictures with his words. We call them parables. If you want to see who God is, read some of Jesus' parables. Look really deep into these word pictures, these snapshots of heaven's glory.

Jesus used parables to give us a glimpse of what he saw for an eternity past, the full glory of our Father God. And you know this because he usually began each story with a little phrase, "The Kingdom of Heaven is like…" It is like a mustard seed, some yeast, or a fishing net. It is like a lost sheep, a lost coin, or a lost son. It is like workers out in the field, a rich ruler in his chamber, or a farmer loading his silos. It is like wheat and weeds, oil and lamps.

A couple of the shortest parables of all are the most profound. I think they get to the heart of what happens when we see God clearly. Instead of being stuck by our situation or self-consciousness, we are filled with a specific hope. That hope moves us.

But first, let's take a look at those parables. "The Kingdom of Heaven is like a treasure that a man discovered hidden in a field. In his excitement, he hid it again and sold everything he owned to get enough money to buy the field. Again, the Kingdom of Heaven is like a merchant on the lookout for choice pearls. When he discovered a pearl of great value, he sold everything he owned and bought it!" (Matthew 13:44–46).

what's with all the buried treasure?

Quick! What does every pirate story have? What do you find at the end of a rainbow? If you catch a leprechaun, what does he have to give you? The answer to all three questions is buried treasure.

For some reason, we have a fascination with buried treasure. It seems like people love stories of digging up an old box, a rusty pot, or a locked chest full of jewels, precious stones, cash money. Even in Jesus' day, this was a big topic of storytelling.

A man named Josephus was a Jewish historian. About forty years after Jesus' death and resurrection, the city of Jerusalem fell to the Romans. Josephus wrote all about it. In one story, he told how the rich landowners all around the great city took their most prized possessions, their most valuable treasures, and buried them underground. They had no way of taking them with them as they fled from their Roman conquerors. The soldiers from Rome discovered some of these treasures. But a few lucky peasants who had remained behind, captured and enslaved by Romans, were also able to find some of this treasure. They squirreled it away and later used it to forge new lives far away in Europe.[18]

About fifty years after the fall of Jerusalem, there was a rabbi by the name of Simeon ben Yohai. Rabbis love to tell stories. Jesus was the greatest rabbi of all, but Simeon ben Yohai was no slouch when it came to painting word pictures. Just take a look at this one. I can't begin to do it justice: "A person…inherited some land that was a manure pile. Now the heir was lazy, and he went and sold it at a very low price. The buyer went to work and dug in it, and in it he found a treasure, and from that he built a great palace."[19]

Isn't that amazing! This big pile of, well, manure held this incredible treasure! No one knew it until this guy decided to dig around in it. Why he decided to dig in it is anyone's guess. But because he did, he found something incredible. In fact, Rabbi ben Yohai went on to explain that this guy was so rich that he was able to hire servants to follow him wherever he went. The lazy heir saw all this and couldn't believe it. That treasure could have been all his—if he had been willing to do a little digging.[20]

We all want buried treasure. I think that's why the lottery is still going strong. That's why the bright lights of Atlantic City and Las Vegas still attract people. We want to strike it rich. Hit it big. Jackpot! But what if we were that jackpot all along? Instead of us looking for treasure, what if we were that treasure? What if you and I were so valuable that someone decided to take all they have and invest it to purchase us?

the treasure hunt

There's a TV show called *American Pickers*. Have you ever seen it? It debuted in 2010 on the History channel. In case you've never seen it, it's like *Indiana Jones* meets *Hoarders*. I guess Indiana Jones was an antique collector, in a way. But his treasures either went into a museum or helped the Allies defeat the Nazis. Anyway, the two guys on *American Pickers* travel the country looking for hidden treasures. They go into people's barns and basements, garages and attics, in search of rare items. I'm not sure how much they make from these trips. The gas and mileage alone would probably make their profits pretty slim. But they love the hunt.

Sometimes they will overestimate an item's worth, spending too much on it. Other times they just can't get the owner to part with their old items and end up empty-handed. And then there are the rarest of times when they hit the jackpot.

Over the years, a few highlights of what they've found include huge circus banners they picked for $700 that netted them an additional $4,300 profit[21] and a huge trove of classic Indian motorcycles from the thirties and forties worth over $62,000 in a brewery in Holyoke, Massachusetts.[22] I want you to put yourself in their shoes for a second. I know that's hard for me. I can't tell the difference between trash and treasure. You set me loose in a little old lady's garage and I would probably just start shoving boxes around. But these guys, the American Pickers, they know exactly what they're looking for. In fact, some say they have a supernatural ability for sensing when they're close to a real valuable hidden in the rubble.

So put yourself in their shoes. You walk down the long, dark steps into a dusty basement with a sea of old, crumbling boxes. You take a deep breath. This is going to be tough. There are more boxes than you thought there would be. And there's only enough light from the single bulb dangling from a power cord in the middle of the room to cast shadows every way you turn. You start to dig.

The first box is old baby clothes, out of fashion a long time ago. The next is half-filled with broken Christmas decorations. Pass. The third and fourth have even less to offer. Then, finally you sense it. You look up from the boxes right in front of you, and a steel lockbox catches your eye. It's on a shelf, the silver glinting against the weak light. You wipe your hands and carefully make your way over to the shelf, dodging an old rocking horse and a weathered chest along the way. The steel box has a rusty lock, but it's not locked. You carefully pull the lid open. You can't see, so you grab the penlight in your pocket. You flick it on and point the beam inside. Your heart stops a moment. There, inside that single little box, is the greatest treasure you've ever found. A cold sweat breaks out on your body. Your throat gets dry. You've only dreamed of finding something this valuable.

You leave the old boxes and bundles and head back up the stairs. You search the kitchen and dining room, desperately looking for the owner. You see her out the window, fiddling around in her garden. You race out the door and run right up to her.

"That was quick," she says. "You were down there less than half an hour. Already giving up?"

"No," you say, trying to catch your breath. "I want it. All of it. I'll buy the whole house."

She stands up from her gardening, an odd look in her eyes. She wasn't expecting this. She has a smile on her face. "All of it?"

You ask for a sale price. She tells you that the house isn't for sale. You tell her that you must have the house and everything inside it. She tells you to make an offer.

You walk a few steps away, take out your cell phone, call up your accountant, and ask one question. "If I liquidate everything right now—all of it—the house, the cars, the shop, the business, I mean everything I own, how much do I have? Including all my bank accounts, my retirement income, my investments. Give me one figure for everything I own."

And he does. You return to the little old lady, who is now looking at her old, faded white house. The shutters need painting. A couple of windows are boarded over. The roof needed to be fixed two decades ago—it's sagging in places. Why would you want to buy this house? You get her attention and give her the figure. "It's all I own. Everything. Please, let me buy this house."

The number is more than she ever thought she could receive in her lifetime. It's more than anyone would ever conceive of paying for a house like this. Are you crazy, or do you know more than she does? Either way, she's a fool if she doesn't take it. She slips a gardening glove off her right hand and sticks it out. "You've got a deal," she says, and you shake on it.

You collapse to the ground, tears in your eyes. You've done it! The biggest score of your career. The one score that will define your legacy and make you rich beyond your imagination! This is like winning the lottery for you. And all it took was giving up everything you hold dear to get it. All it took was bankrupting yourself to get this buried treasure.

who's the treasure, and who's the hunter?

You might think you know where I'm going with this story. You may be wrong. Go back to those two stories Jesus told in Matthew 13. The buried treasure and the pearl of great price. Those are the riches of the kingdom of heaven, and we're the lucky one who came across them. All we have to do is give all we have to secure it.

That's the way you and I have heard those parables explained over and over and over again. I'm not going to pick a fight with Bible scholars or tell church pastors they're wrong for preaching it that way. But what if we took a different look at those two stories? You and I would probably be poor pickers. Okay, maybe a couple of you are good at finding a bargain. But you're not treasure hunters. God is the one who sees you the way you really are. He's the one who can see past the clutter and the trash and the old boxes and, let's be honest, the big pile of manure and find the treasure hidden within.

In that first parable, Jesus said, "The Kingdom of Heaven is like a treasure that a man discovered hidden in a field" (v. 44). Okay, the kingdom of heaven is the buried treasure. You're the one who found it. That seems clear enough, right? But look at this next story: "The Kingdom of Heaven is like a merchant on the lookout for choice pearls" (v. 45). Now the roles are flipped. The kingdom of heaven, which is another way of saying the kingdom of God, is the one on the lookout. Could it be that we've read these two stories the wrong way? What if we got it backward?

You may have been told that your salvation is so precious, of such great price, that you need to be willing to give all you've got to purchase it. It's that expensive! And I agree 100 percent that your salvation is worth a lot. But I don't agree that we pay anything for it. Not even one dime. Salvation is free for those who receive. The Bible makes it clear that eternal life is the "free gift of God" (Romans 6:23). You can't buy your salvation. You can't earn God's love. You can't negotiate God's mercy. You can't purchase an ounce of grace. It's free…for you. For God, it cost him everything.

The most memorized verse in the Bible is John 3:16: "For God so loved the world that he gave his one and only Son, that whoever believes in him shall not perish but have eternal life" (NIV). This tells us that God loved you and me so much that he gave up the most precious thing he had; he gave his own Son. God gives, and we receive. God sells off all he owns, and he purchases us. He is the hunter, and we are the treasure.

Jesus said, "Here's a picture of the kingdom of heaven. A man was out walking one day and found a treasure. It was so valuable that he had to have it. No one else could pay what he could, so he bought the whole plot of land for that one piece of treasure." Jesus said, "Here's another picture. A merchant was out shopping and found a pearl. He could see the value that no one else could. So he sold all he owned just to purchase that one pearl." You and I are the treasure, the pearl of great price. God is the wealthy man who had the resources to purchase us. God saw value that no one else could. And he paid what no one else was able to.

God picked you

Finding buried treasure is hard work. Even with a map, you're never guaranteed to get it. And think about where it's going to be hidden. Not out in the open but in the deepest, most difficult place. Or in some obscure area that no one would imagine.

People have a hard time imagining the buried treasure inside themselves. Whether it's because of low self-esteem or high self-deception, we can miss what should be obvious. We skip right over the things God can see right into. God sees in you something that no one else can see. You can't even see it! But he can. He sees the power you have in your relationships with other people, how influential you can be if you just open up to them and let them open up to you. He sees the success you can be even when you feel like you've failed over and over again. He sees the leader you are, the good friend you've always been, the caring parent you've become, or the loving neighbor whom your neighbor needs.

When we begin an intimate relationship with him, one where he can see us and we can see him, God will begin to reveal those things to us. That's the power of a consistent, personal prayer time. When you begin each day by inviting him into your presence, by reading about him in his Word, and by asking him to go with you each day, you develop a connection to the one who can see you the way you truly are. That's the first step in seeing God for who he is.

Not only did God see in you something that no one else could, but he spent what no one else could. He sees the potential in each human being, but he also knows the deep sin we have in our hearts. We were born with that inside us. We have all sinned, too, and fallen way short of the righteous standard that God's holiness requires (Romans 3:23). When God saw all humanity in that poor condition, he immediately knew the cost. He understood what it would take to get to that buried treasure.

Perhaps you've seen a cross and asked, "Why would anyone kill such a nice man like Jesus?" "Why did he have to go through that?" "Why do I get to be saved and he had to be killed?" This is the whole key. That was the price that had to be paid for our sins. God knew that the price of sin was death. Year after year, men and women tried to pay that price with the lives of their livestock. Lambs and bulls and birds had all been slain to try to make up for the bloodshed that was due for our sins. But they all came up short.

Then, one day, God paid the ultimate price. He took on flesh and died in our place. He paid the price that all of us were unable to pay. He took on our debt and canceled it with his blood. That's the answer of the cross. If there was one word to describe what happened, it would be *paid*. And if you go back to that story, the one of the man walking through the field finding the hidden treasure, you'll see that he paid all he had to get that treasure. If you and I are that treasure, then that means God spent all he had to save us. God bankrupted heaven because he values you so much. He saw the treasure within you and decided it was time to do something about it. He knew he had to have it, and no price was too great for him.

no take backs

If that's the price that God paid, don't you think he would be invested in your life? You don't spend that kind of capital and not make sure you get what you paid for.

Whenever I make a big purchase, like a new 4K TV, I'm going to make sure I get that receipt. What if I get it home and there's something wrong with it right out of the box? I need that receipt to prove to Best Buy that I bought it there and need to return or exchange it. Now let's say I buy a car or a house. When you buy a house, just plan on a full afternoon signing paperwork. And all that paperwork is important. None of us are sure why, but we keep every last page. So imagine the biggest purchase ever in human history, when Jesus paid his whole life for the entire world. Wouldn't you think he would want a receipt? Except he didn't need one. Because there are no take backs when it comes to salvation.

Paul said that God stamps a seal on us, a guarantee, through his Holy Spirit when we trust in him. He also said that there is absolutely nothing that could separate us from the purchase of his love. In other words, no take backs. No returns. No refunds or exchanges. If those are the conditions of the price he spent, don't you think he is invested in your success in life? Doesn't it make sense that he is interested in keeping you from failing?

God's will for you is that you won't fail. He wants to see great things from you. After bankrupting heaven, he's gone all in on your life. He will move heaven and earth to make sure your life matters. We need to start seeing God that way. As a high-end investor buying up all the stock in your life. A man always searching for hidden treasure wherever he goes. A wealthy merchant willing to pay the highest price imaginable. A caring shepherd seeking the last lost sheep. A loving father who gives up all for his children.

Those are the pictures that Jesus painted with his parables. But they aren't metaphors. They aren't some myths of Jesus' imagination. They are all true pictures of the God who sees you. Paul wrote these words to us: "I am certain that God, who began the good work within you, will continue his work until it is finally finished on the day when Christ Jesus returns" (Philippians 1:6).

When we see God the way he is, we see two things. First, we see a God who made us. He created us with utmost care. He took time with each of us, putting passions and gifts and desires right inside us. He made us ready to receive his treasure. He knew what he was doing. But he not only made us; he also moves us. He didn't just create us and let us go. He watches over every moment of our lives. He began a good work, sure. But he will continue working it out within us until we are finally finished. Not tripping over the finish line but triumphantly marching into heaven. And that is the gift he gives to everyone who is in relationship with him.

CHAPTER 14

in relationship with him

You know who God is because someone else who already knew who God is told you about him. Think about it. If you have a relationship with him, it's because someone told you about Jesus. And that person heard about Jesus from someone else who knew him. And that person heard from another person, who heard from another person, who heard from another person who knew Jesus. It goes on and on and on, all the way back to those people you read about in the four Gospels. Those twelve disciples knew Jesus face-to-face. They had a relationship with God in the flesh. And they told people who told people who told people. They showed others what it means to know God and lived in a way that reflected that very special relationship. And eventually that knowledge comes to you.

There was a family in the Old Testament who had a relationship with God. And they showed someone else, a foreigner, what it meant to follow him. They told her all about it. They modeled it with their lives. And when they were gone, she continued following God. Her relationship with God was the result of their relationship with God. And your relationship with God and my relationship with God is a result of her relationship with God too.

a faithful foreigner

In the Old Testament, boundaries were pretty important. They weren't always guarded by armies or walls. Sometimes your ethnic identity was all it took to mark off the boundaries. If you were a Shulamite, for example, you lived over there. If you were an Edomite, this was your place. If you were a Moabite, then you should stay with your own people. And if you were an Israelite, then you had a share of the promised land. You didn't mix with foreigners, and they didn't mix with you. The boundaries might have been invisible, but they were still important.

So it took a lot to cross those boundaries. And that brings us back to that family I was talking to you about earlier. They crossed one of those boundaries. They uprooted from their home in the promised land and moved east into Moab.

Now you need to know something about Moab. The Moabites had their own land and their own gods. While Israel was moving through the wilderness before entering the promised land, the king of Moab hired a false prophet to curse them. God put a curse on the Moabites instead. In Deuteronomy 23, God tells his people to have nothing to do with the Moabites. They weren't allowed into the Israelites' assembly. That included marrying their women. And it definitely meant not moving into Moabite land.

But desperate times call for desperate measures. "In the days when the judges ruled in Israel, a severe famine came upon the land. So a man from Bethlehem in Judah left his home and went to live in the country of Moab, taking his wife and two sons with him." That's how the book of Ruth opens. The famine was so severe that it drove Elimelech and his family from their promise into a land that wasn't their own. In order to survive, they had to make some tough choices.

Along with those choices came consequences. The two sons of Elimelech fell in love with two Moabite women. And since it was love, they got married. With or without God's blessing, we're not too sure. And we don't really get to find out because before too long, tragedy joined their desperation. The father, Elimelech, passed away. Then each son died. They left behind their mother, Naomi, and their wives, both of them Moabites. That was double trouble for poor Naomi.

As a widow without sons, she had no claim to the land she and her husband left behind. If the two sons had remained living, they could take possession. They had that right. But Naomi? She had no rights as a woman. And her two daughters-in-law? They had even fewer rights. As members of the nation of Moab, they would not be warmly welcomed back home in Judah.

Naomi, a follower of God, had found her life turned upside down. She called her two daughters-in-law together, one of them named Ruth, the other named Orpah. She sat them down and explained what lay ahead for them. She told them that she was going to go back home, going to try to find some family who remembered her, who would take her in. But there were no promises.

I wonder if Ruth and Orpah talked it over. I wonder if they walked a little distance away so that Naomi couldn't hear them. Because they had a major decision to make. Would they go with Naomi into this strange, new land? Or would they remain in Moab with their own families, their own nation, their own gods?

I'm sure they recalled all the stories they heard about God. How he had appeared to Abraham and led him from way out east to a land of promise. Maybe they heard the stories about God showing Abraham the night sky, asking him to number the stars if he could. That would be the number of Abraham's descendants. I can imagine them expecting that they, too, would be part of that number now that they belonged to Naomi's family. I'll bet Ruth and Orpah retold the stories of Moses and Aaron meeting God in the wilderness, learning his name. Perhaps they thought of Joshua and all the judges. Maybe they recited parts of the Law their husbands had taught them. "Listen, O Israel! The LORD is our God, the LORD alone. And you must love the LORD your God with all your heart, all your soul, and all your strength" (Deuteronomy 6:4–5).

But now they had to decide. Would they stay, or would they go? What lay ahead of them was a lot of uncertainty. But it would include chasing after this God they'd heard about. It would mean choosing to be in relationship with a God who wanted to be in relationship with them. They came back to Naomi, who explained it carefully to them. "Go back to your mothers' homes…May the LORD bless you with the security of another marriage" (Ruth 1:8–9).

Orpah listened, and she turned away from Naomi. She returned to her people. But Ruth heard something else. She realized that staying close to Naomi meant remaining in relationship with God. So she agreed to go with her mother-in-law. No matter what was ahead of her, she knew that God would be there. And that was who she really wanted.

let's get one thing clear

Can you imagine yourself in Ruth's shoes? I can't. How do you make that big of a decision, one to leave your home and everyone you know and go to such an uncertain place? It's the type of decision that used to keep me stuck in one place, unable to move. But Ruth was resilient. She saw things differently from Orpah and even Naomi, it turns out. And because of her ability to see spiritually, she was able to move spiritually. She was decisive. She rebounded. She moved ahead in confidence. Why? Because she saw one thing clearly.

Along the way in this book, we've talked a lot about how we see things. We started by looking clearly at our situation. Then we moved on to how we see ourselves. You may think that we should have started with how we see God. But that was all by design. There was a method to my madness, not a madness to my method. I've experienced this over time, that how we see our situation and ourselves will determine a lot about our lives. It actually drives us to seeing one thing crystal clear. But before we get to that, let's walk through that whole process in the life of Naomi.

Naomi and Ruth headed out from Moab on their way back to Bethlehem. When they arrived, they found out that squatters had taken over their old homestead. They no longer had a claim to it. And since Naomi's husband and sons had died, she had no male relative to help her out. But the women of Bethlehem didn't care. They just wanted to see Naomi. They ran out and greeted her by name in the street. And what was her response? "'Don't call me Naomi,' she responded. 'Instead, call me Mara, for the Almighty has made life very bitter for me'" (Ruth 1:20).

You see, *Naomi* means "pleasant." I'm sure that was a great name growing up. Just think about how her husband responded when he asked her for her name the first time. Pleasant. *That's the type of girl I want to marry*, he must have thought. But now, she didn't want that name anymore. She got a new name—Mara. What does *Mara* mean? It means "bitter." She'd been through some tough times and no longer felt pleasant. She let bitterness settle in her heart.

How you see your situation can affect how you see yourself. That's what it did for Naomi. And it can happen to you too. If you have a distorted picture of your past experiences, you may find yourself growing a root of bitterness. And that will never be helpful in life. When our situation overwhelms us, we tend to turn inward. We begin to paint ourselves as the victim. "I can't believe this has happened to *me*!" And instead of getting our sights set right on our situation, we allow it to cloud how we view ourselves.

But the next step is even worse. How you see yourself can affect how you see your God. Once your self-perception gets clouded, you tend to let that bitterness turn toward the Lord.

Here's what Naomi had to say about that. "I went away full, but the Lord has brought me home empty. Why call me Naomi when the Lord has caused me to suffer and the Almighty has sent such tragedy upon me?" (Ruth 1:21).

Every victim has an offender. Why not let it be God? *He was the one who got me into this situation. He was the one who let this happen to me.* Naomi had felt full, pleasant, loved, and cared for. Sure there was a famine back home. But they were making the best of it in Moab. But then tragedy struck. And it was God's fault. Or at least that was how she saw it. Now she couldn't take one more step. She was drained, completely emptied by God. She was suffering.

When we get a wrong view of our situation, it distorts all other views. When we have a bad self-image, it can affect how we see God. Instead, we need to refocus. Allow who God is to inform who you believe you are. That's the key to freedom and the power to move forward.

refocus

Do you remember those Magic Eye posters? When I was a kid, they were really popular. It was a bunch of squiggly lines and waves and blobs. But if you looked at it just right, you could see a 3D image appear. I never could get it to work right.

I had friends who helped me out. They could see it, but I couldn't. They finally told me how to put my face really close and then back up a little bit at a time, focusing on a point right in the middle. Suddenly, I saw it! A picture of a shark came to life right in front of my eyes. I blinked, and then it was gone. But I saw it, even if only for a split second.

It took someone who could see it to help me see it. And it was a trick of focusing my eyes just right. When we can see the picture clearly, it's only because we've refocused our sight. What does it take to see God clearly? What does it mean to see who he is to those in relationship with him? It's all about that refocusing.

Paul loved all the churches he helped start, but I think there was a special place in his heart for the church at Philippi. At least you get that sense when you read the letter he wrote them. He was very encouraging, he was motivating, and he talked a lot about the love and joy of being in relationship with God. He saw something in them the first time he met them. And as their relationship with God grew, he knew he needed to help them keep focused on who their heavenly Father truly is.

The first part of the letter, the salutation as it's known, is full of these great words of encouragement. "Every time I think of you, I give thanks to my God" (1:3). "Whenever I pray, I make my requests for all of you with joy" (v. 4). "I am certain that God, who began the good work within you, will continue his work until it is finally finished on the day when Christ Jesus returns" (v. 6). I don't know about you, but I need a Paul in my life, someone who sees the good work God is doing inside me and encourages me to keep moving.

How did Paul accomplish this? What's the route that he suggested the Philippians take to keep focused on God? How could they refocus after some bad circumstances? Or clear up any doubtful self-image? He put it in the form of a prayer: "I pray that your love will overflow more and more, and that you will keep on growing in knowledge and understanding. For I want you to understand what really matters, so that you may live pure and blameless lives until the day of Christ's return. May you always be filled with the fruit of your salvation—the righteous character produced in your life by Jesus Christ—for this will bring much glory and praise to God" (vv. 9–11).

You may think the point of this prayer is "knowledge and understanding." That must be it. That's the way we keep focused. If we can only get into our head who God is and how he sees us, then we'd be able to dowse our doubts and walk in confidence.

But that's not it. Maybe it's about bearing fruit. Just buckle down and get to work. Focus on the good work you're supposed to do every day, and that will keep you in tune with him. Listen, I'm not going to say you shouldn't do good things. But I think that comes after the more important part, the part that really matters.

Paul prayed for one thing to increase in them: love. It's an agape love. That's a special kind of love. It's the type of love that leads you to lay your life down for others. Isn't that what Ruth did? Her husband was gone. Naomi freed her from any responsibility, any debt she had to the family. Ruth was free to leave her. But instead, Ruth loved her. It was an agape love that led her to say, "Wherever you go, I will go; wherever you live, I will live. Your people will be my people, and your God will be my God" (Ruth 1:16).

If you want to know more about God and understand his ways better, it begins with agape love. If you want to live "pure and blameless lives," then it has to start with agape love. If you want to be a person of character, make sure you are rooted in agape love. If you are hoping to bear good fruit in life, you can't accomplish that without agape love. If you want to live a life of praise to God, unless you have agape love, they'll just be empty words.

give, pray, fast

How do we get to that place of agape love? What does it take not only to let it overflow but just to begin to live that type of life? It may seem odd to some of us, to lay down our lives for others. But it's exactly what Jesus did. It's what Ruth did too. It's the example for all of us.

In the first sermon from Jesus recorded in Scripture, I think he gives us the key. You see, ever since the giving of the Law on Mount Sinai, this idea of agape love has been central to following God. In Deuteronomy 6, one of those same passages I'm sure Ruth's in-laws quoted daily, Moses gave the nation of

Israel a simple prayer to pray. It's all about love. "Love the Lord your God" (v. 5).

But the people of Israel had a hard time fulfilling that. *What does it really mean to love? Whom do I love? Are there people I can hate?* And Jesus cleared the air: "You have heard the law that says, 'Love your neighbor' and hate your enemy. But I say, love your enemies! Pray for those who persecute you!" (Matthew 5:43–44).

Now the people listening probably had a lot of questions for Jesus. "Wait, are you sure? I really have to love my enemy? But what if they've been really, really mean to me? How do I even start to do that, Jesus?"

And Jesus anticipated those questions. In the very next breath, Jesus turned to three areas that are designed to tie your heart to God's heart. You see, God loved all of us. Even when we were out of relationship with him, and even when we were enemies of God, he loved us enough to send us his Son to die for us (Romans 5:10). So he knew what agape love was all about. He knew what it took to let that love overflow from within to others. He knew that it was the key to understanding who God is, to truly seeing him for what he means to those who are in relationship with him. So he laid down these three things: give, pray, fast.

- "Give your gifts in private, and your Father, who sees everything, will reward you" (Matthew 6:4).
- "When you pray, go away by yourself, shut the door behind you, and pray to your Father in private. Then your Father, who sees everything, will reward you" (v. 6).
- "When you fast, don't make it obvious…Then no one will notice that you are fasting, except your Father, who knows what you do in private. And your Father, who sees everything, will reward you" (vv. 16, 18).

I don't think Jesus randomly said these things. There was a point to this, a progression of ideas and actions. He wanted us to know the secret of loving our neighbors and our enemies. He wanted us to see how loving God would overflow to the world around us. He wanted us to follow in that same pattern of agape love that he laid out.

The first thing we do is give. The first step of love is to give something. It has to be something of value though. John 3:16 says that God showed his love by giving his Son. Remember, he bankrupted heaven for you and me. There's no way we can match that level of giving, but true agape love starts with us trying.

Next, we pray. You might see prayer as a chore or a discipline. The less we pray, the less we want to pray because we may think that God is upset with us for not praying. But prayer is not about keeping a list or checking a box. Prayer that refocuses us on God is agape prayer. When we pray because we love God, we will find ourselves getting closer and closer to him.

Finally, we fast. Fasting is to give up eating for a time. It's about putting your flesh in check. It's the physical act of laying down your life for others. There's no better way to express agape love than to put what is most important to you on the line. Paul said the key to overflowing agape love is understanding what's really important. When we fast, we're saying there is something more important than even food.

i've got a secret

Take a look again at those three passages from Matthew 6. What do they all have in common? The word *private* is in all three. Another translation is "secret." God wants to share a secret with you. This isn't the secret to life. It's not a secret recipe. It's not secret knowledge or hidden wisdom. It's a secret place.

All throughout Scripture, this whole idea of a secret place shows up over and over and over again. In Job 22, we hear about the secret place where God dwells. Psalm 139:15 tells us that he formed us and made us in that secret place. And in Psalm 27, we call out with David for God to bring us into that secret place.

So now Jesus tells us that we can come into that secret place. It's where God shares his presence and rest with those who are in a relationship with him. It's where he reveals himself. We give in secret. We pray in secret. We fast in secret. Not because showing the world would cancel out any blessing. But because coming into that place of rest is the blessing itself.

Ruth knew this. When Naomi's family came to Moab, something was different. They were a family who lived in the secret place with God. And Ruth could sense it. Maybe every other neighbor knew it too. There was just something different about them. And Ruth wanted that secret. In fact, she told us exactly why she couldn't stay at home, why she had to go with Naomi back to the promised land, to Bethlehem: "Your people will be my people, and your God will be my God" (Ruth 1:16).

In other words, she wanted to be a part of that secret place of God. She got a glimpse of it, and now she wanted even more. She could see who God truly is to those who are in relationship with him. She wanted that same relationship. Naomi had lost that sense of the secret place. She was so exhausted that she couldn't find rest. She was so depressed that she couldn't feel his presence. But Ruth still knew there was something more.

Naomi allowed her circumstances to determine how she saw God. Ruth let her calling determine how she saw God. She found herself in that secret place of rest with God, and it drove her to go further. And she did! Over the rest of the story, Ruth found someone who could help her and Naomi, a distant relative who could redeem the claim on the land. All he had to do was marry Ruth. In the end, like every other good romance story, the two get married, settle down, and start a family.

Remember how I said your relationship with God is tied directly into Ruth's relationship with him? Well, here's how that happens. The last verses of Ruth give the details of Ruth's family. She had a son named Obed. And Obed grew up, married, and had a son named Jesse. That same Jesse later became the father of David. King David.

And it was through David's line that Jesus himself came to earth. The promised King, the world's Savior, the Messiah himself. His many-times great-great-great-grandmother was a Moabite who knew nothing about God. But she learned by seeing those who were in a relationship with him. She got a sense of that secret, a secret that begins and ends with self-sacrificing agape love. And that secret defined who she was.

How will you define yourself? How will you see God? If you are in a relationship with him, are you seeking him in that secret place of rest and presence? If you aren't in a relationship with him, are you ready to begin that part of your life? The answer to your calling is just on the other side of seeing God clearly.

CHAPTER 15

seeing God behind the scenes

"Once you see it, you can't unsee it." Have you ever heard that before? Many times, it refers to something you really don't want to see. Sometimes you've seen a picture a million times, and then you see that one detail that changes the whole thing. Your perception shifts, and you can't shake it. Or maybe it's an optical illusion, like one of those Magic Eye posters I mentioned earlier. It looks like a bunch of swashes and lines and zigzags until one day, the picture comes into clear view. You finally see it. You have to train your eyes to pick it up. But once you do, you can see it every time.

We need to train our eyes to see God. We need to discipline them against seeing God for who he isn't. We need to concentrate on seeing him for who he is. And we need to zero in on how he lives with those who are in relationship with him. We need to train our eyes to see a God who is invisible. That can be really hard. When you can't see God, it's easy to forget he's there. Out of sight, out of mind. Or so the saying goes. When we fail to see him, we can get stuck. We can't move. We're frozen in our tracks. So we need to find our eyesight again.

Here's the problem. Most of the time, we assume that God is hiding. We think that the invisible God is purposely obstructing our view of him. Some divine game of hide-and-seek. And he's a great hider. When we encounter circumstances in our lives that seem insurmountable, we begin to think that he's gone on vacation. He's nowhere to be seen. He's left the building. When we focus on our faults and failures instead of our future, we begin to think that he's left us behind. He's done with us. He's cutting his losses. And if you think that God's invisible nature is proof of either of those things, then you're wrong. I'm sure of it. Because I used to think that way—until I started seeing him, really seeing him, behind the scenes.

It's the God behind the scenes we need to learn how to see if we want to mature in our faith. We get a glimpse of his glory all around us before we come to know him. We get a fuller picture when we come to know him as Savior and Lord. But it's when we start to see him moving just under the surface of our lives that we are really moving in our faith.

"i'm feeling lucky"

When I was a teenager, DSL internet existed but not where I lived. Fiber was not even thought of yet. We had dial-up. It's a super slow internet that teenagers today have never experienced. It would make crazy noises, sounding like a warship in SOS mode.

My brother had received a basketball recruitment interest letter from Central Christian College. I had never heard of it, and neither had he. But I had heard of Google. So to the internet I went! I typed in the first two words of the school: "Central Christian." I started to hit search, but something led me to click a different button, the "I'm Feeling Lucky" button.

Now I'm not going to say it was God—but I'm not going to say it wasn't him either. You see, the "I'm Feeling Lucky" button is like betting all your search engine chips on one click. Normally, you punch in a word or phrase and hit search. A list of thousands and thousands and millions of websites will come up, ranked according to the most relevant. But the "I'm Feeling Lucky" button will give you one shot to get it right. You're banking that Google knows the one site in the whole World Wide Web you want to go to.

I clicked it. I didn't get the college. Instead, I landed on the front page of Central Christian Church in Las Vegas, Nevada. For the first time my eyes were open to relatable Christianity.

Churches in the rural part of Missouri where I grew up were lucky to have a bi-vocational pastor. Most of the time they were good-hearted volunteers. The musicians did not always know how to play the instruments they played. And the piano was probably out of tune. Maybe the singer too.

As the site began to load, I felt like I was looking at a mistake. I thought, *There is no way there is a church in Sin City.* I saw a church that was making a difference in a context that I knew needed it. As a fifteen-year-old, I was in awe. There was a video that explained what the church was. It simplified God's great entity into four things: plug in, charge up, live out, pass on. Their video was not about style. It was about a church that understood the components of the local church according to Matthew 28 and Acts 2. I was hooked.

I found another video. This one showed their senior pastor, Jud Wilhite. He talked about his need for God. He was on drugs before, but God changed his life and chose to use him as a teacher. He talked about how he became the pastor. He said six words that I was not sure a pastor had the authority to say. It was a new way of thinking for me, as my exposure was limited.

"It's okay to not be okay."

I knew that I had to do something to bring this way of thinking into my context. I was not sure how I was going to do it or even if I could, but I committed to trying. I began to study what I found on Jud and what he was doing in Las Vegas to increase the church's kingdom impact. I found a few of his sermons and downloaded them, even though downloading the sermons took several days each. This enabled me to watch them whenever I wanted to and not have to worry about waiting for the video to load in the future. I typed them word for word and studied when he interjected cultural relevance and how he stayed true to biblical accuracy. I practiced what it would look like in my context.

I looked at their model of the church. The plug in, charge up thing. Church had always felt like a chore to me before, but now it was giving me life. Before online church was cool, I was a part of one from rural Missouri. God was giving me eyes to see what it looked like to be a part of a difference-making church. He was stirring my faith and ordaining my steps.

Several years later, a mutual friend said he had someone he wanted to introduce me to. His name was Bart Rendel. Bart was looking for a young millennial who understood the local church and social media. He wanted someone to help with a new ministry he and a partner were pioneering. It was a great opportunity, and I hit the ground running.

The ministry is called Intentional Churches. They partner with local congregations to help them double their kingdom impact by installing a church operating system. Over the past six years, dozens of churches on the Outreach 100 lists for largest and fastest-growing churches have installed this operating system. This includes three of the top five fastest-growing churches in the United States.

I felt lucky to have the conversation with Bart. My mind was blown when I found out Bart's background as the executive team pastor at Central Christian in Las Vegas. He served there for twelve years until he took the operating system he helped architect and turned it into Intentional Churches. I told him that for years his church was influential in my understanding of the local church. The plug in, charge up videos were still on my computer.

Bart scripted those videos and had them made. It felt like God had been wiring up this connection for many years prior to our meeting. God began preparing me for his work even when I was a teenager.

turn on a lamp

If you want to see clearly, you turn on a light. It's a no-brainer. So when God wants us to see him, he's going to be found among some lamps.

At the end of the Bible, in the book of Revelation, you'll find the clearest picture possible of God. He shows up in all his glory. He's sitting on a throne, worshiped by angels and elders and living creatures. He's there riding on a white horse, his Word like a sword as he flies across the sky for all to see. He's resting in the end, in New Jerusalem, lighting up the whole world with his glory.

You see him clearly at the end of the book, but he's there right now if you can find him, if you're looking behind the scenes. And John told us where we can see him. "When I turned to see who was speaking to me, I saw seven gold lampstands. And standing in the middle of the lampstands was someone like the Son of Man" (Revelation 1:12–13).

That Son of Man is Jesus Christ, God in the flesh. He was visible for any to see during his lifetime, during those years covered by the Gospels. And he will be visible for all to see at the end of this world and the beginning of the next. But today, he is visible somewhere else. Among the lampstands. What exactly are the lampstands?

I know there are lots of images and pictures and visions in the book. And some of them are kind of hard to understand, to interpret. In fact, thousands of people over thousands of years have given their own opinions about the different scenes unfolding in that book. But this picture of the lampstands is one we absolutely know. It's the church. "This is the meaning of the mystery of…the seven gold lampstands:…The seven lampstands are the seven churches" (Revelation 1:20). Each lampstand is a church. There were seven that John originally wrote to, so he saw seven lamps. But in the time since then, that number has increased and increased. There are thousands of lampstands. Everywhere and anywhere on earth that God's people gather to worship his Son, the Holy Spirit is shining like a beacon, calling out to any who would hear.

The church is the visible glory of God in the world today. If you want to see God, just look for a church. If you're wondering where God is when tragedy strikes, look for his people. In nearly every natural disaster, you will find church people coming to help. You will see the glory of God, not revealed through those terrible problems. You'll see him right there, helping through the hands of his people. When you see the church, you see God.

But there's more to it. What did John see exactly? He saw Jesus behind the scenes. He saw him walking among the lampstands. That's where Jesus is. Right in the midst of our churches. That's how he works.

Have you ever seen that TV show *Undercover Boss*? They take a boss or a CEO or a company president and dress him or her in a disguise. The boss pretends to be a regular worker, sometimes a new employee learning the basics. They give the boss some lower position in the company and put them right to work. And the boss learns all about the employees, their problems and challenges, and then the boss makes some changes. They find out what's really going on under the roof of their own business and are motivated to do things a little differently.

The whole idea of *Undercover Boss* is that the boss is so out of touch with what's really happening that they have to fool everyone just to figure it out. They have to disguise themselves to check up on their employees, to really get to know them.

I think we sometimes think that God is an undercover boss. Sure, he's in our churches. But maybe he's in the back row checking things out. Or he's just offstage making sure we hit that note just right during worship, that we give enough in the offering, that our sermons are theologically correct and spiritually compelling. He's got a checklist in his hand and a mustache and glasses on so we don't recognize him.

But God is anything but an undercover boss. He's front and center every time we meet. He's showing off in our worship. He's moving in the hearts of givers. And he's honored by our sermons. He may not be visible to our natural eye, but he's there in our spiritual sight line. And he's at work. Behind the scenes doesn't mean out of the action. In fact, that's right where the action is!

Every time I get a new Blu-ray disc, I like to check out the special features. The movie is the point, of course, but once it's over, I like to flip through the menu to see what else there is. The deleted scenes are cool. And the interviews can be interesting. But what's really great are the behind-the-scenes clips. The behind-the-scenes clips tell you what it's really like to shoot a movie, weave in computer graphics, and tell a story. It's how moviemaking works.

If you want to know how the church works, you have to go behind the scenes. That doesn't mean that you sit in on a staff meeting, help out a pastor with sermon prep, listen in on a pastoral counseling session, tag along on a hospital visit, play along with worship practice, or pull up a chair backstage or in the green room to get the inside scoop. That's not behind the scenes. Not really. The real behind the scenes of church is when Jesus starts moving among the lampstands.

If you want to know how the church works, you'll find it when you hit play on the behind-the-scenes clips of Jesus displaying his glory. When John saw those lampstands, it was more than just a nice picture. It was an image that meant something. It meant that the church was working like it should. And the secret was Jesus, God behind the scenes.

what's it going to take?

Back in college, I did feel stuck. I wasn't sure where I was headed or what impact I could make. But as I looked for God in my life, sitting on the red beanbag chair and listening to Jesus Culture, God showed up. The love I felt rush over me was so strong. The only way I can describe it is how Lydia experienced the Lord in Acts 16. *The Message* Bible says she felt "a surge of hospitality" (v. 15). Her experience with God changed her trajectory. She used what the Holy Spirit had deposited into her to build the local church. Out of that surge, the church of Philippi was born in her living room.

The love I felt rush over me was so strong that it covered the years of my life where that sensation was void. I knew what God could offer wasn't just for me, but it was for everyone. It was a turning point for me. I realized God was asking me to share his love with every person I would come across. So I decided to go all in on this ministry thing. I felt inadequate and underqualified. But when I took a step back and looked from a different perspective, I knew what I wanted to do. That's because I had been watching God behind the scenes. I saw how he used unlikely people in extraordinary ways.

Did you know that those lampstands didn't show up for the first time in Revelation? In fact, hundreds of years before, another prophet got a behind-the-scenes view of God. His name was Zechariah. And he saw those same lampstands.

An angel awoke the prophet from a dream. He had a new message for the prophet, a new vision to see. What did he see? A golden lampstand with a bowl full of oil on top. And what did it mean? Let's see what the angel had to say: "It is not by force nor by strength, but by my Spirit, says the LORD of Heaven's Armies"

(Zechariah 4:6). Lampstands. God behind the scenes. Jesus in his church. The Holy Spirit on the move. That lampstand is the glory of God but in a very specific way.

Churches want to get noticed. In fact, I work with a lot of churches looking to make an impact online through social media. There are a lot of tools to get in front of people who may be interested in your church. If you're not a believer and you want to check out this whole God thing, the first place you may go is Google. You might hit that "I'm Feeling Lucky" button. You may go on Facebook or even Instagram. So I work with churches to make sure their online presence is nice and clear. If you're a church, getting noticed is important.

But just having a great website, a dynamic video clip, some good photos, and relevant content isn't enough. Not by a long shot. You need to give people a reason to show up. No one is going to attend your church because your logo looks sharp. They're looking for a reason that goes deeper. Church is church when the people of God are moved into action. We need to be men and women who are willing to reach out to the unreached. We need to be willing to touch the untouchable. There are people within the reach zone of every one of our churches who don't know about God. They see their situation and are concerned. They see who they are in their sins and are convicted. They need to see a God who loves them, who gave up everything for them. And they can only see that when we show them grace.

So think about that vision that Zechariah got. It was not a vision of a group of believers stuck where they were. They weren't intimidated by their past. They weren't frozen by their self-perception. They were resilient and moving. Why? It's not because of how great they were.

"It is not by force." You can't move people forward by forcing your beliefs on them. That doesn't mean we give up on our convictions. It means we help convince them of the value God sees in them.

"Nor by strength." When you try to do it all on your own, you will burn out fast. You may get a few victories under your belt. But putting the entire load on your shoulders is a horrible vision.

"But by my spirit, says the LORD." It's up to God and God alone. If his Spirit is not present in our churches, our churches will be going nowhere fast.

Here's the truth. God doesn't need us to force ourselves on the world. We just shine the light of God, and he will call those people to himself. And he doesn't need our strengths either. God doesn't rely on our abilities. He is counting on our obedience.

When we obey God and depend on the Spirit, our churches are transformed. We may have a good run if we work really hard at it. We may get pretty far actually. But eventually we run out of steam. And we'll stop dead in our tracks. Depending on our own strength won't get us where we need to go. But putting all our faith in God, depending on Jesus for everything, and tapping into the true power that comes from the Holy Spirit are the only ways that any of us and all of us together as the church can ever hope to get anywhere.

CHAPTER 16

getting on God's frequency

For us to step into the next level of what God has for us, we must understand that God speaks in quiet places.

Did you know we can hear better than we can speak? It's true! The human voice can speak and hear within a small slice of frequencies. Sound is measured in hertz. Not the car rental company, but it's spelled the same. The average male voice is 80–180 hertz; the average female voice is 165–225 hertz.[23] In fact, some women—and this was on *MythBusters*, so you know it's true—can actually break glass with their voices.[24]

That's one range of using our voice, but our range of hearing is even wider! God designed our ears to hear as low as 20 hertz and as high as 20,000 hertz.[25] Sound below that is called infrasonic. Those frequencies have the power to produce headaches and has the potential to be weaponized.[26] Sound above that is called ultrasonic, what doctors use to see your baby before he or she is born.

What does any of that have to do with what we're going to be talking about? Simple. We are designed to be better hearers than speakers. God gave us two ears and only one mouth, right? So he intended for us to listen twice as much as we talk. And our range of hearing, the frequency, is much wider than our range of talking.

Frequency is the wavelength that allows you to hear clearly. That's what we're going to be talking about. Getting on God's frequency and hearing him. And the bottom line is this: if we are having trouble hearing God's voice, it's not that he's doing a bad job of speaking; rather, it's that we're doing a bad job of listening.

Jesus, very boldly, told us in Luke 8:8, "Anyone with ears to hear should listen." He gave us ears to hear. Mark Batterson says in *Whisper: How to Hear the Voice of God*, "Learning how to hear the voice of God is the solution to a thousand problems."[27]

You may think that not hearing God's voice is just one of a hundred spiritual questions or issues you have. But I think this is the *one* issue we face. Because if we could learn this, then all our other spiritual questions, issues, and problems would be solved. Hearing God's voice is how we understand God.

Maybe you have felt stuck because you haven't been able to hear God. I'm going to share with you a simple but strong prayer for unlocking this in your life. If you've ever said, "I can't hear God's voice," this simple prayer is for you.

But first, why don't we hear God's voice? I think there are two things people say. First, "God doesn't talk today." They think he only spoke in the Old Testament and the New Testament. He said all he had to say in the Bible. Those things don't happen anymore. Secondly, "God doesn't talk to me." This is the belief that God talks only to pastors or super-spiritual people. *He would never talk to me because I'm so messed up. He has better things to do than talk to me.* Neither of those things is true.

speak, Lord

I want to look at two stories of people in the Bible hearing God's voice: Samuel and Elijah. "Meanwhile, the boy Samuel served the LORD by assisting Eli. Now in those days messages from the LORD were very rare, and visions were quite uncommon" (1 Samuel 3:1). Samuel was probably around seven or eight at this time. If you think that God talked nonstop in the Bible and then shut it off today, that's not what this says. Maybe you don't hear God's voice because you aren't expecting it. Samuel was just a young kid. No one would expect the God of the universe to speak to a kid. What restrictions are you putting on God's voice that you need to take off?

> One night Eli, who was almost blind by now, had gone to bed. The lamp of God had not yet gone out, and Samuel was sleeping in the Tabernacle near the Ark of God. Suddenly the LORD called out, "Samuel!"
>
> "Yes?" Samuel replied. "What is it?" He got up and ran to Eli. "Here I am. Did you call me?"
>
> "I didn't call you," Eli replied. "Go back to bed." So he did. (vv. 2–5)

Samuel heard God's voice but thought it was Eli talking to him. Sometimes we don't hear God's voice because we don't recognize it. Maybe he is talking to you. Maybe he is sharing with you what your destiny is. But you don't know because you don't know what to look for.

> Then the LORD called out again, "Samuel!"
>
> Again Samuel got up and went to Eli. "Here I am. Did you call me?"
>
> "I didn't call you, my son," Eli said. "Go back to bed."
>
> Samuel did not yet know the LORD because he had never had a message from the LORD before. So the LORD called a third time, and once more Samuel got up and went to Eli. "Here I am. Did you call me?"
>
> Then Eli realized it was the LORD who was calling the boy. So he said to Samuel, "Go and lie down again, and if someone calls again, say, 'Speak, LORD, your servant is listening.'" So Samuel went back to bed.
>
> And the LORD came and called as before, "Samuel! Samuel!"

> And Samuel replied, "Speak, your servant is listening." (vv. 6–10)

We don't hear God's voice because we're just not asking him to speak. God responds to simple prayers. It's not some super-spiritual formula or some special preparation you have to go through. "Speak. Your servant is listening." How great is that?

a whisper

> "Go out and stand before me on the mountain," the LORD told him. And as Elijah stood there, the LORD passed by, and a mighty windstorm hit the mountain. It was such a terrible blast that the rocks were torn loose, but the LORD was not in the wind. After the wind there was an earthquake, but the LORD was not in the earthquake. And after the earthquake there was a fire, but the LORD was not in the fire. And after the fire there was the sound of a gentle whisper. (1 Kings 19:11–12)

Those phrases stick out to me. "But the LORD was not in the…wind…earthquake…fire." That tells me that many times we have this expectation of how God is going to speak. We don't hear God's voice because we put our own expectations on him.

"When Elijah heard it, he wrapped his face in his cloak and went out and stood at the entrance of the cave" (v. 13). A whisper…a still, small voice. It's barely audible. Why a whisper? Elijah had to get close to God to hear him. Elijah had to get quiet to hear him.

Sometimes the world is too loud for us to hear God. We need to shut out the competing voices in order to hear God's voice. Sometimes our life is too loud for us to hear God. We need to turn off the TV, shut down our phone, get alone with God, get quiet before him, and then we can hear him clearly. Sometimes, our own schedule is too cluttered for God to get a word in edgewise. We go from one event to the next, afraid we're going to miss out. But what we're really missing out on is God's voice.

A part of our brain filters all our sensory intake—what we hear, what we feel, what we see, and so on—all except smell, which goes straight to our cerebral cortex. This part of our brain is very advanced and can tune out certain things we don't need or don't think we need. That's why a mom can ask her son, "Did you not see your socks on the living room floor?" No, he didn't. His brain totally filtered it out. But this part of our brain works to filter out sounds and noises. That's why a car alarm can go off, and eventually, we get used to it and don't hear it anymore. That part of our brain is shutting down that noise.[28]

I wonder if we've allowed that part of our brain to shut off the voice of God. It takes getting close to God and getting quiet to hear him. Do you have a set time and place daily to hear God's voice? Let me give you two concepts we need to get right in order to hear God's voice. These are two things we can do that will get us on God's frequency.

1. set the atmosphere

Guys, when your girlfriend or wife wants to talk, you'd better get ready. Men can have a conversation anywhere while doing anything. Women need to set the atmosphere. She may say, "Let's talk," while we're on the phone. Okay, let's talk. Isn't that what we're doing right now? But what she means is, let's find a time and place where you can get on my frequency.

But it's not all about what she wants. If a wife needs to talk to her husband, she'll set the atmosphere. She may plan his favorite dinner, have him sit down and watch SportsCenter while she prepares it, and after dinner, go to the living room, have him sit in his favorite chair, and maybe even rub his feet. "So remember how I told you last month we need a new washer and dryer? Well, today they both broke. And the ones I want are $1,500 each." She knows what to do to set the atmosphere and get on his frequency so he can hear her.

We need to make sure we're setting the atmosphere for God to talk to us and for us to listen. This is about setting a time and a place to hear him. Setting a time means being consistent and placing it as a priority on your calendar. Don't let anything else take that time. Setting a place means finding somewhere free from distractions. Planning to hear God's voice in a busy coffee shop or restaurant? Nope. That's why Jesus talked about going into your closet to talk to him.

In Luke 10 there's this great story of two women who were close to Jesus. "Her sister, Mary, sat at the Lord's feet, listening to what he taught. But Martha was distracted by the big dinner she was preparing. She came to Jesus and said, 'Lord, doesn't it seem unfair to you that my sister just sits here while I do all the work? Tell her to come and help me'" (vv. 39–40).

Mary set the atmosphere. She sat at the Lord's feet, the position of a disciple. Martha was distracted. She thought what she was doing was good. But it kept her from what was better.

2. give him your attention

When Elijah was in desperate need of a word from God, he first had to give the Lord his undivided attention. It would have been very easy to hear God in a windstorm, an earthquake, or a firestorm. But God wants your attention, so he whispers.

We treat prayer like a one-way conversation sometimes. We do all the talking, and God does all the listening. We've got a list of stuff to say or ask for. And then we wonder why we can't hear God's voice! We're not giving him our attention. We're doing all the talking.

We all know people like this. They talk and talk and never listen. How annoying is it to have a conversation with them? Or with those who aren't listening. They're just waiting for you to stop talking so they can start again. God wants to have a conversation with you. But he never talks to just hear himself talk. He always talks with a purpose.

> I will show you what it's like when someone comes to me, listens to my teaching, and then follows it. It is like a person building a house who digs deep and lays the foundation on solid rock. When the floodwaters rise and break against that house, it stands firm because it is well built. But anyone who hears and doesn't obey is like a person who builds a house right on the ground, without a foundation. When the floods sweep down against that house, it will collapse into a heap of ruins. (Luke 6:47–49)

It's not those who hear God's voice who build a good foundation. It's those who hear God's voice *and then act on it*. Maybe we don't hear God's voice because he knows we're not ready to do what he's going to ask us to do. What did God tell Samuel? He told the boy that he was about to make good on his warning to Eli by killing his sons because of their wicked behavior (1 Samuel 3:11–14). Tough words for an eight-year-old! But God knew Samuel was ready to hear it. What did God tell Elijah? He gave him step-by-step instructions for who to anoint, who to find, and who would take care of Ahab and Jezebel. And Elijah followed those steps to the letter.

> The LORD told him, "Go back the same way you came, and travel to the wilderness of Damascus. When you arrive there, anoint Hazael to be king of Aram. Then anoint Jehu grandson of Nimshi to be king of Israel, and anoint Elisha son of Shaphat from the town of Abel-meholah to replace you as my prophet. Anyone who escapes from Hazael will be killed by Jehu, and those who escape Jehu will be killed by Elisha! Yet I will preserve 7,000 others in Israel who have never bowed down to Baal or kissed him!" (1 Kings 19:15–18)

Our receptiveness to God's voice will only rise to the level of our willingness to be obedient. Don't expect your revelation to exceed your obedience. Don't expect God to talk to you if you're not ready. The book of James is blunt about it: "Don't just listen to God's word. You must do what it says. Otherwise, you are only fooling yourselves" (1:22).

a conversation starter

We need a conversation starter with God. I told you at the beginning of this chapter that I would give you a simple prayer to help you hear God's voice and get on his frequency. Here it is:

Speak, Lord. Your servant is listening and ready to respond.

That's it. Very easy. You can remember it without even writing it down. Make a point to find a time and place each day to be with God. It's okay to talk, but make sure you've set the atmosphere and given him your attention. Listen to him. Then say this prayer. Don't say it and wait thirty seconds, then decide, "Well, I guess he won't talk to me." It may take some time and patience and consistency and persistence. Do this every day if you want to hear God's voice.

God whispered to me

I spent a season of ministry working from outside the church. I traveled and spoke at conferences. Sometimes I was a digital media consultant, developing websites and helping with social media strategy. It was also the early days of Intentional Churches, and I was helping to build that ministry. This was one of the most fruitful and exciting seasons of ministry I have had so far. However, I started to feel like it was time to work at a church again. I had been really successful in student ministry. This seemed like the obvious and natural alignment for me. In no time, I had been given several different opportunities without me even applying. Many of them were at the largest and most successful churches in the United States.

However, God was nudging me somewhere else. The Holy Spirit was leading me to a smaller church in a very rural part of southern Illinois. I had spoken there before at a big youth conference they held. A few months later, a staff member contacted me and asked me if I would consider being their senior pastor. Immediately I politely declined. I was only twenty-five years old and had no desire to be a senior pastor.

A couple of weeks later, I realized through prayer, fasting, and sleepless nights that God was calling me to that church. I reconnected with that staff member and told him what God had spoken to me. He was very excited. They invited me to preach the very next Sunday morning. And several more Sunday mornings following. Eventually it became my full-time position.

On the surface, no one in my inner circle agreed with me taking the position in McLeansboro. In a side-by-side comparison with some of the other opportunities in front of me, it did not seem like it was the best fit for my desires or skill set. Some in my family implored me to take a different position at a more famous church in a city somewhere else. But this opportunity was from God. It is better to have one opportunity from God than a thousand amazing opportunities from someplace else.

Almost two years into being the senior pastor, I began to hear stories of this phenomenal revival that took place at the church in 1970. Hundreds were saved, and people from many different states attended as it went on for forty-nine consecutive days. As I dug more into the research about it and the church's history, I learned that God raised up some world-class leaders during that time. One of those who announced his call into ministry at that revival was Randy Clark.

I had never heard of Randy Clark before then. His incredible history began at McLeansboro First General Baptist. His father was a deacon, his mom volunteered faithfully, and he was involved in the student ministry. He was in a tragic accident and, at age eighteen, encountered a miraculous healing of his own. This would lead him on the adventure of a lifetime. He writes in depth about his early experience at McLeansboro First General Baptist in his book *The Essential Guide to Healing*, written with Bill Johnson. Later, God used Randy to birth the revival that broke out in Toronto, Canada, in January 1994 that continued six nights a week for over twelve years.

Randy is best known for the gift on his life for activating and imparting gifts of the Holy Spirit. The late John Wimber was the first to recognize this grace on Randy's life. John heard the audible voice of God tell him twice that Randy would one day travel the world laying hands on pastors and leaders to activate and impart to them gifts of the Spirit.[29] Randy also continues to demonstrate with great tenacity the Lord's power to heal the sick.

While having been used to launch several famous ministers into the new level of their anointing by laying hands on them and prophesying to them, the focus of his ministry is on the average person in the congregation, encouraging that they, too, can be used by God through the gifts of the Spirit, especially words of knowledge and gifts of healing. His message is simple: "God wants to use you." Some say that Randy is the most influential Christian minister in our lifetime.

Randy lived in Pennsylvania, where the ministry he founded, Global Awakening, is headquartered. However, some of his family still had a home in Hamilton County, Illinois, where I lived. I noticed on his website that he would be in my region leading a service at a nearby church. I decided to attend that service, and I would never be the same.

There were four hundred people or so in attendance. As Randy began to preach and share incredible healing testimonies, people all over the room began to experience healing. By the end of the service, at least eighty people had encountered some type of healing. One person had been unable to open his hand for many years. After God touched him, I watched as he shook his son's hand for the first time. They were both overwhelmed with tears and God's goodness. This was my first time ever experiencing the power of God in this way.

Randy invited me to spend some time eating with him in the green room after the service. I was so intrigued as he told stories of what he has seen in fifty years of ministry, since that revival in McLeansboro in 1970. He gifted me with about ten of his books and told me the order in which I should read them. Most of them were on healing and the supernatural work of God. I read them in the order he suggested. I have always held some reservations about the charismatic movement. Some of it I don't understand. Parts of it have seemed excessively emotional or even suggestive. I did not encounter that with Randy. He was activating the supernatural without being spooky. As I read his books, I grew hungry for more. I wanted to see God show up like that in my own ministry. If the incredible power of God like this is available, then I want to access it.

In the early summer of 2019, Global Awakening and Randy were hosting a conference called "Signs, Wonders, and Church Growth." Because of my work with Intentional Churches, I was drawn to the church growth part of the conference. I was still apprehensive about the charismatic movement, but this conference seemed safe to me. Plus the pastor who hosted the healing service where I first met Randy was a featured speaker at the conference.

The conference was great. Nothing spooky happened. I did not encounter anything that conflicted with my General Baptist theology. I was inspired to hope and believe for more. Soon after the conference, a good friend of mine and a crucial volunteer at our church was diagnosed with a rare form of cancer growing between her heart and lungs. Doctors said the tumor needed to come out as soon as possible and scheduled surgery soon after.

Her name was Julie. She worked as an elementary school teacher. She was the first person I baptized sideways due to a separate rare condition she has in her back. Months before this diagnosis, she was receiving experimental treatment at the National Institute of Health in Washington, DC. I flew to the hospital (straight from a conference in Honduras, where I had been speaking) and was there for several days as she recovered in the ICU. After everything she had just gone through, I could not believe that she was facing the big C.

At the same time of her diagnosis, my cousin Jesse and his friend Brayden were visiting. Jesse often spends time with me during summer, sometimes an entire month at a time. His friend Brayden had recently moved in with Jesse's family, so he came along this time too.

When they arrived in McLeansboro for their summer visit, Jesse told me that Brayden was an atheist. Beyond that, he had even burned Bibles in the past for fun. I asked Jesse, "Did you tell him that I am a pastor? We are going to be going to church like five times a week." We had three services on Sunday, prayer meeting on Monday, prelaunch services for a new campus on Tuesday, high school youth on Wednesdays, and junior high youth on Fridays.

"I told him," Jesse said.

Brayden did not say much the first few days he was around me and the people of my church. I could tell it was a brand-new experience for him. I asked Brayden what it would take for him to believe that God was real. He said, "I guess if I saw a miracle."

To make things a little easier on Brayden, Julie invited the boys to skip some of the church stuff I was doing and hang out on her daughter's farm. They could swim, ride the side-by-side around, and fish. She grew attached to them, and they grew attached to her.

Then Julie was diagnosed with cancer. We were all heartbroken. The day before Julie had her presurgery appointments,

Jesse, Brayden, and I, along with about ten others, gathered around her for prayer. This was the first chance I really had to put into practice some of what Randy had been teaching me.

We declared in the mighty name of Jesus for all cancer to go. We prayed that we believed Jesus paid the price for our healing because Scripture says, "He was beaten so we could be whole. He was whipped so we could be healed" (Isaiah 53:5). We believed Julie was healed. The next day in her presurgery appointments, the cancer had significantly decreased in size. Her doctors canceled the surgery! A couple of weeks later, she had another checkup. All signs of the cancer had completely disappeared. There was no residual evidence whatsoever. The medical professionals were shocked. We were not. Jesus does what only he can do!

This was the miracle that Brayden needed to see. When we found out that Julie's surgery was canceled and the cancer was disappearing, I went into the bedroom of my house where Brayden was staying. He said he had never seen anything like this. He decided in that moment to accept Jesus as his Savior. He would never be the same.

Since that moment with Julie, I have encountered dozens and dozens of others who have received supernatural healing. One of the most notable stories is about Kimbria Blake. She was a student at Harvard finishing up her doctorate degree. These are her words:

> Without the supernatural strength, willpower, grace, and peace only He can provide, I would have undoubtedly failed to complete this thesis. For the last four years of my thesis I suffered immensely with several severe chronic pain issues, the worst being fibromyalgia and occipital neuralgia that made every single part of living excruciating. Even a slight breeze on my skin would have me crying! Completing my thesis and writing this

> dissertation was one of the hardest things I've had to do. I can only attribute the strength others see in me to the underlying current of joy and happiness that comes from trusting in the Lord—even when I was desperately holding on to the last threads of His garment with all of my strength. In that I would like to thank God for bringing two amazing men of God into my life the past six months, Tyler Feller and Joshua Silverberg, who have been diligently praying for my healing (nothing medical was working!). Miraculously on August 7, 2020, after waking up in immense pain, as they prayed with me, I was completely healed of all pain, PTSD (from an abusive marriage) and chronic bodily suffering in too many forms to list. I now look forward to finding a job after I defend (I was thinking I'd have to move back home) and discovering all of the things I can now do! His timing is perfect![30]

This was included in her dissertation that was approved by the Division of Medical Sciences at Harvard University. This amazing activation of gifts and belief for the supernatural was imparted to me by the Holy Spirit through Randy Clark.

On December 2, 2019, I felt God speak to me. Isaiah 22:22 says, "I will give him the key to the house of David—the highest position in the royal court. When he opens doors, no one will be able to close them; when he closes doors, no one will be able to open them." I sensed in my Spirit that God was saying, *Tomorrow I am going to open a door for you, and I want you to walk through it.* I had been praying that prayer for several months: *Speak, Lord. Your servant is listening and ready to respond.*

December 3 came, and I said yes to everything the entire day, even if it was something small. For example, my friend Tony called me and asked, "Do you want to go to lunch?"

Excitedly I said, "Yes!" He made note of my overenthusiasm for lunch that day, something we did together several times a week.

Later that afternoon I received an email from Randy with the subject "Invitation to education and relationship with Randy." It was an invitation for his mentorship. He felt like God was calling him to invest in the next generation of pastors and church leaders in this season. Somehow, God chose me to be a part of this. I replied back, in part saying, "I felt the Holy Spirit speak to me last night and say today that he was going to 'open a door for me, and I was to walk through it.' I feel I need to be obedient to this opportunity based on my prayer experience yesterday."

Had I listened to my inner circle around me, I may have never moved to McLeansboro, met Randy Clark, and been exposed to the supernatural power of God. Would God have healed Julie from cancer? Would Brayden have encountered a miracle that led him to repentance and salvation?

One thing I know is that God is always working behind the scenes. He is persistently pursuing people who don't know him. He's constantly talking. The best days of your life are just around the corner. He is opening doors for you that no one can shut. He has a purpose and destiny for you that goes above and beyond anything you can imagine.

Don't stop. You're too important. You're too important to God's plan. You're too important to your friends and family. You're too important to your church. You have made it this far, so don't stop now. Say this simple prayer with me, and I believe you will begin to see the impossible dreams in your heart come to life, just like I have.

Speak, Lord. Your servant is listening and ready to respond.

And when you hear him speak, respond in obedience.

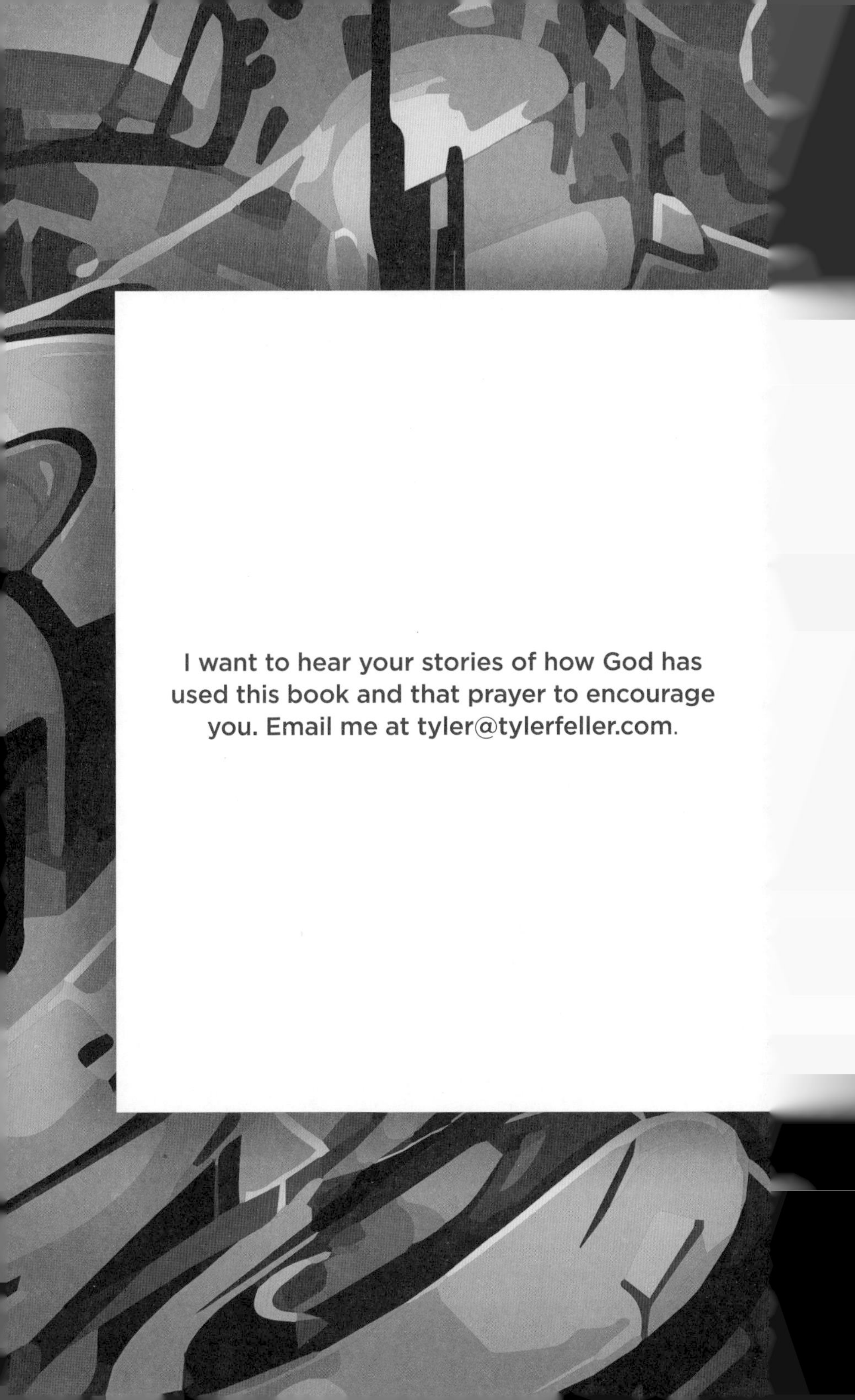

I want to hear your stories of how God has used this book and that prayer to encourage you. Email me at tyler@tylerfeller.com.

endnotes

1 Ashley Haugen, “When Bad Things Happen to ‘Good’ Families,” StyleBlueprint, January 19, 2020, https://styleblueprint.com/everyday/lexie-smith-human-trafficking-survivor/.

2 “Blindness and Vision Impairment,” World Health Organization, October 3, 2022, https://www.who.int/news-room/fact-sheets/detail/blindness-and-visual-impairment.

3 Dennis Pollock, “John Newton, Author of ‘Amazing Grace,’” Spirit of Grace Ministries, accessed January 27, 2023, https://www.spiritofgrace.org/articles/nl_2018/00_newton_john.html.

4 Willie James Jennings, *Acts*, Belief: A Theological Commentary on the Bible (Louisville, KY: Westminster John Knox Press, 2017), 237.

5 Elizabeth L. Maurer, “Washington and the French and Indian War,” Mount Vernon (website), accessed May 11, 2023, https://www.mountvernon.org/george-washington/french-indian-war/washington-and-the-french-indian-war/.

6 Allie Caren, "Why We Often Remember the Bad Better than the Good," *Washington Post*, November 1, 2018, https://www.washingtonpost.com/science/2018/11/01/why-we-often-remember-bad-better-than-good/.

7 Delilah Gray, "The Real Reason Katy Perry Changed Her Name," *The List*, May 28, 2021, https://www.thelist.com/423779/the-real-reason-katy-perry-changed-her-name/.

8 "Michael Keaton Biography," IMDb, accessed January 30, 2023, https://www.imdb.com/name/nm0000474/bio.

9 "Kirk Douglas Biography," IMDb, accessed March 20, 2023, https://www.imdb.com/name/nm0000018/bio/.

10 Ron Charles, "How Dr. Seuss's 'Oh, the Places You'll Go' Became a Graduation-Gift Cliché," *Washington Post*, May 29, 2019, https://www.washingtonpost.com/entertainment/books/how-dr-seusss-oh-the-places-youll-go-became-a-graduation-gift-cliche/2019/05/29/c584fe8e-8021-11e9-95a9-e2c830afe24f_story.html.

11 "Famous People Who Found Success after 40," Finance 101, January 20, 2023, https://www.finance101.com/success-after-40/.

12 Mark Batterson, *The Circle Maker: Praying Circles around Your Biggest Dreams and Greatest Fears* (Grand Rapids, MI: Zondervan, 2016), 44.

13 Kevin M. Kruse, "How Corporate America Invented Christian America," *Politico*, April 16, 2015, https://www.politico.com/magazine/story/2015/04/corporate-america-invented-religious-right-conservative-roosevelt-princeton-117030/.

14 Charles Haddon Spurgeon, "The Dream of Barley Cake," The Spurgeon Center for Biblical Preaching at Midwestern Seminary, sermon given November 22, 1885, https://www.spurgeon.org/resource-library/sermons/the-dream-of-barley-cake/.

15 "Tony Dungy," Pro Football Hall of Fame, accessed May 11, 2023, https://www.profootballhof.com/players/tony-dungy/.

16 Charles Duhigg, *The Power of Habit: Why We Do What We Do in Life and Business* (New York: Random House Publishing Group, 2012), 61–65, Kindle.

17 *Black Panther*, directed by Ryan Coogler (2018; Burbank, CA: Marvel Studios), 134 minutes.

18 Flavius Josephus, The Jewish War VII.1.V, http://penelope.uchicago.edu/josephus/war-7.html.

19 Marvin W. Meyer, *The Gospels of the Marginalized: The Redemption of Doubting Thomas, Mary Magdalene, and Judas Iscariot in Early Christian Literature* (Eugene, OR: Wipf and Stock, 2012), 59n186.

20 Meyer, *The Gospels of the Marginalized.*

21 *American Pickers*, season 3, episode 1, "A Banner Pick," aired December 6, 2010, on History Channel.

22 The Republican Entertainment Desk, "'American Pickers' Dig up Treasure in Springfield, Make Biggest 'Pick' in Series History in Holyoke," Masslive, April 24, 2014, https://www.masslive.com/entertainment/2014/04/american_pickers_dig_up_treasu.html.

23 Kenneth Estrada y Santiago, "EQing Vocals: What's Happening in Each Frequency Range in the Human Voice," Flypaper, July 8, 2020, https://flypaper.soundfly.com/produce/eqing-vocals-whats-happening-in-each-frequency-range-in-the-human-voice/.

24 *Mythbusters*, season 3, episode 18, "Breaking Glass," directed by Alice Dallow, aired May 18, 2005, on Discovery, https://go.discovery.com/video/mythbusters-discovery/breaking-glass.

25 Estrada y Santiago, "EQing Vocals."

26 Tia Ghose, "A Sonic Attack in Cuba? How an Acoustic Weapon Might Work," *Live Science*, August 11, 2017, https://www.livescience.com/60110-how-sonic-weapon-might-work.html.

27 Mark Batterson, *Whisper: How to Hear the Voice of God* (New York: Crown Publishing Group, 2017), 2.

28 Anne Trafton, "How We Tune Out Distractions: Neuroscientists Trace a Brain Circuit That Filters Unwanted Sensory Input," MIT News, June 12, 2019, https://news.mit.edu/2019/how-brain-ignores-distractions-0612.

29 Randy Clark, *The Essential Guide to Healing: Equipping All Christians to Pray for the Sick* (Ada, MI: Baker Publishing Group, 2011), 25.

30 Kimbria Justine Blake, "*Staphylococcus aureus* Activates Sensory Neurons in the Skin to Cause Pain or Itch during Infection" (PhD diss., Harvard University Graduate School of Arts and Sciences, 2020), xviii, https://www.proquest.com/openview/4fba6a77c45d3998aac66059fb35bdae/1?pq-origsite=gscholar&cbl=18750&diss=y.

about the author

Tyler Feller is the president of Tyler Feller Ministries, a global not-for-profit corporation that exists to raise up the next generation of leaders through coaching, consulting, curriculum, and conferences.

Tyler is a passionate pastor excited about all God is doing. At Movement Church, he serves as the lead pastor, helping ignite a unique and growing community on fire for Christ. He hosts a podcast called *Deep Waters* that features some of the most influential Christian leaders of our time.

Tyler has been featured as a guest speaker at conferences, camps, churches, and business meetings in every region of the US and several nations globally. He graduated with a master's degree in business management and attended seminary at Global Awakening Theological Seminary.